Where Is God in War?

A Look at War through the Eyes of Sackie Kwalalon

Sackie Kwalalon and Dr. Doug Collier

Lens & Pens Publishing, LLC
Auburn, WA
All rights reserved.
ISBN-10: 069291305X
ISBN-13: 978-0692913055

Cover Design and Maps—Caroline Brumfield
Author Photos—John Keay
Content Photos—Nathan Jones

DEDICATION

We dedicate this book to our wives, who understand our passion for the children of Liberia and uphold it; to all donors to Serve the Children, who make it possible for the children of Liberia to achieve their hopes and dreams; and to the blessed memory of Pastor Dennis Gaye.

CONTENTS

ACKNOWLEDGMENTS

When we first undertook this project in 2006, the Liberian Civil War was too fresh in our minds, and we had to set it aside. Later, our friend Skeeter Wilson, of Lens & Pens Publishing, encouraged us to pursue it to completion. And with the tremendous help of our editor, Trevor O'Hara, this project was finished. This was a team effort; thank you, Skeeter and Trevor, for making it all possible.

We also had a team of friends who continued to encourage us through the year-long process of writing, researching, and many times experiencing memories we did not want to remember. Thank you for your help, Zac Barnes, Erica Bronk, Caroline Brumfield, Erin Herried, Angela McGovern, Heidi Otis, Kelly Swaleson, Sheilagh Todd, and all our other friends who read early drafts of our manuscript and made suggestions.

FORWARD

I never before had the desire to write or co-write a book. Never. In 1997, I had a very comfortable life as a CPA. I had a young family, and I was active in my church. Life was good. Then God prompted me to go to Liberia in West Africa. And a mysterious thing happened: I listened to Him and went.

In Liberia, I became involved with an amazing man of God named Sackie Kwalalon. I helped to start a nonprofit organization, All God's Children, to educate child soldiers in Liberia, and Sackie became the head of our schools there. At first, our relationship was more as employer and employee, and for several years, we maintained this professional relationship until our traumatic experiences together during the Liberian Civil War. Now, Sackie and I have become brothers, not just in Christ, but true brothers in every sense. There is nothing we would not do for each other.

This book is about Sackie's life—from his birth in Yowee, Liberia, in 1964 to the present. As we chronicle his life, we look at the history of Liberia from its founding by freed American slaves in 1820 through the vicious Liberian Civil War that raged from 1989 to 2003. We highlight the founding of the All God's Children school system and look at the future of Liberia. We answer the question, "Where is God in war?"

This is the story of my brother and best friend, and I hope it touches your life as he has touched mine.

Dr. Doug Collier

Education is simply the soul of a society as it passes from one generation to another.
—G.K. Chesterton

AUTHOR'S NOTE

I should be dead.

Many times throughout my short time on earth, I should have died. Doug Collier and I, Sackie Kwalalon, have often asked ourselves this question: "Why are we alive?" We remember the experiences we had during the fourteen-year Liberian Civil War and wonder why God allowed us to survive when so many others did not.

We lived and others died. Is this fair? What about the families who no longer have a husband or a father? Should they consider themselves unlucky, while we should consider ourselves the lucky ones? You might think we should be happy we lived through these terrible events, but this is not always the case. The truth is, we live each day with the memories. We live with the nightmares.

You will see as you read this book that I have come to know why I am still alive. But the answer does not make the memories any easier to deal with; grief and trauma take time to heal. On my regular trips back to Liberia, I have many good memories as I drive through Monrovia and the rest of the country, but many places also remind me of other times I would just as soon forget. I still shudder from the flashbacks I have when I pass by some of these places. Even though the war ended in 2003, it is still very difficult for me to talk about my life during the war. There is no telling how long this will last.

When the Liberian Civil War started in 1989, there were around 2.5 million people from sixteen different tribes in Liberia spread out over a country the size of Tennessee. By 2003, around 250,000 people had been killed in the war, and most of them were innocent civilians, and the US Department of State estimates 700,000 refugees fled from Liberia during the war to escape the fighting.

This means over one third of the Liberian people were either killed or had to run away from our country to save their lives and their families. It is easy to read quickly over numbers, but these are real people. Doug knows some of them, and I know many more. So many died, and some of those who survived have never been able to discover what has happened to their loved ones.

Liberia and her people were devastated by this war:

- Most medical clinics and hospitals shut down: 242 out of 293 public health facilities were looted or forced to close during the fighting.[1]
- Prior to the start of the war in 1997, there were 400 trained medical doctors in Liberia, but by the middle of 2003, only 20 doctors remained in the country.[2]
- There is still little electricity or running water and no garbage collection, internet, or land-based telephone system following the war.
- Seventy-five percent of schools were destroyed.[3]
- During the fighting, 30 percent of children under five suffered from malnutrition, and 22 percent of children died from diarrhea, due to lack of clean water and medical care.[4]
- An estimated 10 percent of children were recruited or forced into militias and were given drugs and alcohol to numb them toward violence, and 10 percent of children also suffered the horrifying trauma of seeing their families and friends assaulted, tortured, and murdered.[5]

Can you imagine what it would be like in the United States to go through a war like this for fourteen years? One third of the people killed or running away to escape the US. The infrastructure destroyed. Child soldiers high on drugs and alcohol killing people. And no relief in sight, only more fighting, killing, and running.

In the US, we sometimes get upset when someone cuts us off on the freeway. We yell at them and maybe gesture. I have seen drivers speed up next to a car that cut them off and give the other driver the *glare*. This seems a bit silly in the grand scheme of things, when I saw more dead bodies in one day during the war than I will

---

1. United Nations, World Bank, and National Transitional Government of Liberia, "Joint Needs Assessment," February 2004, 51.

2. Joseph Saye Guannu, *Liberian History since 1980* (Monrovia: Star Books, 2010).

3. United Nations Humanitarian Division, "Liberia CAP 2006," October 3, 2005, 21.

4. United Nations Office for the Coordination of Humanitarian Affairs, "Liberia CAP 2006," November 30, 2005, 14.

5. CIA, The World Fact Book, "Liberia," last modified June 15, 2017, https://www.cia.gov/library/publications/the-world-factbook/geos/li.html.

see live people most days now.

All of us experience some kind of hardship or loss in this life. Whether we have experienced war, family tragedy, or some other loss, we come to a place where we ask, "Why?" And when this happens to me, I eventually take a breath and thank God for the life He gave me. The answer to my why question is God Himself. I believe He has a perfect plan for my life. Doug also believes He has a perfect plan for his life.

I do not know how many friends and relatives I lost during the Liberian Civil War. Some were killed in the fighting, some died from malnourishment, and some probably died alone in the jungle fleeing from their homes. Some died because they became sick and could not access medical help. But many more lived through the war, including my wife and children. How many more would have died if God had not kept the evil of war in check?

Second Thessalonians 2:7 states that God is in fact restraining lawlessness in this world: "For the secret power of lawlessness is already at work; but the one who now holds it back will continue to do so till he is taken out of the way (NIV)." I give Him all the praise for doing this. When we ask why God allowed this fourteen-year civil war to happen, we also need to consider all the years we lived in peace in Liberia. God also allowed those years. Why should God be blamed for everything that goes wrong and never receive the praise when things go right?

All of us have bumps along the road of life. Some bumps can be very big, and we wonder why, we wonder where God is in the tragedies. In these times, do we trust in God, or do we trust only in ourselves?

As you read my story, you will see that I had a lot of big bumps on my road. Maybe some of you will be able to relate to them. I hope the rest of you will never experience the big bumps I lived through. But along my road of life, I came into a personal relationship with Jesus Christ that resulted in the forgiveness of my sins and the reward of eternal life, now and when Jesus restores heaven on earth. Christ has promised me an abundant life, a life that is full and has a purpose (John 10:10). And you will see in my story that I have struggled with this.

Why did God allow me to live when so many others died? Because He has a plan for my life. I do not know every aspect of that plan, but I know He does, and I can have peace knowing that

He is in control. God never promised me a life of ease, but He did promise me that He will always be with me wherever I am. He has never broken that promise.

Where was God during the Liberian Civil War? Right beside me, where He always is.

INTRODUCTION: THE HISTORY OF LIBERIA

Many people do not know the history of Liberia, that my country is America's stepchild. Liberia's history began in the United States in 1817, when a group of influential Americans, led by James Monroe (the fifth President of the United States), Francis Scott Key, Henry Clay, Andrew Jackson, and others, formed the American Colonization Society for the purpose of sending freed American slaves to Africa.[6] At the time, there were over 108,000 freed slaves in the US, while the total population of the US was estimated at 7.2 million people.

The members of the American Colonization Society had mixed reasons for the group's formation. Slave holding members wanted to remove freed slaves from the US out of fear. They were afraid that freed slaves would influence other slaves with their ideas of freedom, which could lead to revolts such as the slave revolts in Virginia of 1800 and 1802 or a larger revolt similar to what the French experienced in Haiti. The slave holding members were also concerned about potential economic ruin, because much of the farming economy was based on slavery and the labor it provided. Other members of the society, mainly Quakers, wanted to evangelize Africa. Their goal was to send freed slaves to Africa so they could lead the natives there to a saving knowledge of Christ.[7]

The idea of giving freed slaves their own country was not a new idea. In 1787, Great Britain started resettling former American slaves who were freed to reward their loyalty to the Crown during the American Revolution. They were settled in the African country now called Sierra Leone. However, neither the slave holders nor the evangelists of the American Colonization Society considered the reality of the situation. Originally, African slaves came from many different regions of Africa, and the now freed slaves were more American than African. Most of the freed slaves had been born in America and had no knowledge about life in Africa—nor

---

6. Claude A. Clegg III, *The Price of Liberty: African Americans and the Making of Liberia* (Chapel Hill: The University of North Carolina Press, 2004), 32.

7. Clegg, *The Price of Liberty*, 33.

did they have the immunities to certain African diseases, such as malaria and yellow fever, that their ancestors had developed. And many freed slaves did not want to leave the United States due to the hardships they knew they would face in Africa. They felt that, even though they experienced substantial discrimination in the US, it was their home and they were at least free.

Nevertheless, a ship carrying seventy-seven former American slaves left the United States for Africa in 1820. The ship landed on the west coast of Africa in what is now the country of Sierra Leone,[8] where many of the Americans succumbed to malaria. Eventually, they decided to move to a more hospitable area, and they sailed south, landing on an island in what is now the Mesurado River on the African coast, which they named Providence Island. Later they moved to a larger neighboring island in an attempt to escape the mosquitoes on Providence. This new island they named Bushrod Island, after George Bushrod Washington, the nephew of George Washington and a US Supreme Court Justice and then President of the American Colonization Society.

After some years, with a $100,000 grant from the US Congress, these former American slaves purchased a thirty-six mile stretch of land on a hill overlooking a small harbor across the river from Bushrod Island. The colonists named the colony Cape Mesurado, and they named the city they built there Monrovia (Village of Monroe), after the US president, James Monroe. Monrovia was to become, eventually, the capital of Liberia.[9]

By 1835, thousands of freed slaves from America arrived and formed five more colonies surrounding Cape Mesurado. These six colonies eventually merged, and the country of Liberia was formed. On July 26, 1847, Liberia declared itself an independent nation, and the Liberian constitution was drawn up along the lines of the US constitution. However, the Liberian constitution denied voting rights to the indigenous people of Liberia. This was not to change until 1946.

Liberia means "Land of the Free" (*liber* is Latin for free). Liberia is an English-speaking country, and the country's currency is the Liberian dollar (though the US dollar is often preferred). The

---

8. Phil Waite, "The American Colonization Society," last accessed May 5, 2017, http://personal.denison.edu/~waite/liberia /history/acs.htm.

9. US Department of State, last modified July 13, 2016, http://www.state.gov/r/pa/ei/bgn/6618.htm.

Liberian flag is based on the US flag: It has eleven stripes, representing the eleven men who signed the Liberian Declaration of Independence. The red and white symbolize courage and moral excellence. The white star represents the freedom the founding ex-slaves were given, and the blue square represents the African mainland. There are only two countries in modern Africa that were never colonies of a European power: Ethiopia and Liberia.

When independence was declared in 1847, there were 6,100 people of American descent living in Liberia. The new country was immediately recognized by Great Britain, France, and most other European countries.[10] However, the United States did not recognize Liberia as a country until 1862, when Abraham Lincoln was president. This is because, in America at the time, racism was widely believed to be an insurmountable problem, and many Americans could not accept that black people and white people are equals. This has always been a source of confusion for Liberians, because America is our parent country.

In 1878, the Americo-Liberian colonists formed the True Whig Party, and no organized political opposition to this party was allowed. Indigenous Liberians lived mainly in the interior, away from Monrovia, and they revolted against the elected government of the colonists many times between 1856 and 1980.

In 1926, Henry S. Firestone Sr. negotiated a ninety-nine-year lease of one million acres of Liberia, and the Firestone Natural Rubber Company, a subsidiary of the Firestone Tire Company of Akron, Ohio, was given concessions by the Liberian government to establish the largest rubber tree plantation in the world at what became Harbel, Liberia. At the time, British companies controlled about 80 percent of the production of rubber in the world, 70 percent of which was consumed by America.

The rubber industry has played a great role in the economy of Liberia. The supply of rubber became extremely important to the Allies during World War II, after the Japanese overran the rubber tree plantations operated by the British in Asia. During World War II, the US constructed the airport Roberts Field (named for the first president of Liberia) near Harbel and the seaport that serves Monrovia, called Freeport, on Bushrod Island. By 1950, rubber

---

10. Marran Fraenkel, *Tribe and Class in Monrovia* (London: Oxford University Press, 1970), 16.

sales constituted 40 percent of Liberia's national budget, and by 1971, Liberia was the largest exporter of rubber in the world, as well as the third largest exporter of iron ore.

This is how Liberia came into being, and the seeds of discontent were sewn from the beginning. Americo-Liberians dominated the social order. They spoke only English, they built churches and houses in the American style, and they created a cultural and racial caste system with themselves at the top and indigenous Liberians at the bottom. Indigenous Liberians were not allowed to engage in government, run businesses, or hold any high-profile positions. Few indigenous Liberians were allowed an education. Most were farmers, street vendors, and members of the army. Though, indigenous Liberians who did join the army most often saw their promotions blocked by Americo-Liberian officers.

William Tubman was the nineteenth President of Liberia from 1944 to 1971. He was an attorney from the coastal town of Harper and created Africa's first one-party state, where the entire country was incorporated into one vast True Whig patronage machine controlled exclusively by Tubman. Literally all those who held government positions were appointed by Tubman, and any government expenditure greater than $250 was personally approved by Tubman.

Tubman increased the access to education for all Liberians, and indigenous Liberians gained the right to vote during his administration. However, few indigenous Liberians were given a true opportunity to improve their status, because they were still considered second-class citizens. Almost 100 percent of registered voters remained Americo-Liberians, and all political opposition to the True Whig Party continued to be suppressed.

Tubman extended trade concessions to foreign investors and was paid large royalties for these rights. However, these funds were not invested into improving the infrastructure of the country but were used to import American goods, so the elite Americo-Liberians could maintain an American lifestyle.

President Tubman died in 1971, when I was seven years old, and he was succeeded by his vice president, William Tolbert Jr. Tolbert saw the need for political reform to accommodate the increasing number of educated young people who were not Americo-Liberians. Indigenous Liberians now wanted access to higher government positions that had long been held only by

Americo-Liberians. Tolbert also took a less pro-American position in foreign affairs than Tubman, and this impacted his relations with the US government, particularly the CIA, whose West African headquarters were in Liberia.

Tolbert was president of Liberia from 1971 till April 12, 1980, when he was shot and skewered with bayonets by seventeen noncommissioned officers of the Liberian Army, all indigenous Liberians. The conspirators, none of whom had even a high school education, killed twenty-seven people in the Executive Mansion, along with the president, and ordered the arrest of ninety of Tolbert's officials. This bloody coup was led by a twenty-eight-year-old master sergeant named Samuel K. Doe.

On April 22, 1980, Doe ordered the execution of thirteen of Tolbert's arrested officials, mostly cabinet members, after they were found guilty by military tribunal of corruption, high treason, and gross violation of human rights. The men were tied to wooden stakes on the ocean beach behind the Barclay Training Center barracks in Monrovia and shot to death by a firing squad as thousands of Liberians watched and cameras rolled. Their bodies, along with the body of President Tolbert, were carted through the streets of Monrovia for all to see.

President Tolbert's death put an end to the True Whig party. Doe and his supporters established the People's Redemption Council (PRC) and took over administration of the country. They declared themselves the indigenous sons of the soul of Liberia—they were the first leaders of Liberia who did not trace their ancestry back to the United States. Descendants of former American slaves had dominated the political and economic power of Liberia for over 130 years, and within two weeks, the new indigenous rulers established a reputation for brutality and lawlessness. Americo-Liberians were arrested at whim and paraded naked through the streets of Monrovia where crowds of onlookers pelted them with insults and stones.

Africa is no stranger to coups, but the bloody and public manner in which government leaders and others were killed in 1980 established a new low for Liberia in the eyes of the world. The PRC began systematically murdering all Americo-Liberian leaders and anyone who was against the new regime. They claimed they represented the true people of Liberia and were saving the country from the elite Americo-Liberians. Shortly after taking power, the PRC banned all political activities and opposition. Doe was from the Krahn tribe, which then represented about 5 percent of the Liberian population, but within a few years, at least one-third of positions in the central government were held by Krahn tribesmen. This was only the beginning of Liberia's troubles.

Sackie Kwalalon and Dr. Doug Collier

1 ~ MY EARLY YEARS

I was born unto the blessed union of Sackie Kwalalon Sr. and Nowah Galamue Kwalalon on July 29, 1964, in the small village of Yowee, Liberia. My birth name was Nandeh, which means "Black Father." There are sixteen indigenous tribes in Liberia, and my family is from the Kpelle tribe (pronounced *pay-lay*). Yowee is located outside of Gbarnga, the capital City of Bong County, and was home to about one thousand people at the time of my birth. Gbarnga is a very important crossroads in the Liberian interior where roads from Northern Sierra Leone and Monrovia intersect.

In Yowee as a child, eight members of my family lived in a three-room mud hut. My parents had nine children, four boys and five girls. I am the third child of my parents and the second son. My older brother, John Sackie, was the first child of my parents, followed by my sister, Yamah Sackie. As a child, I could be very troublesome—many times, instead of doing my chores (fetching water from the river, watching my younger siblings, gathering firewood), I would run off and play with my friends—but John and Yamah and my parents were always there for me. John died in 1996, during the war. Yamah died after the war in March 2009.

As a child in Yowee, I was very close with my parents. However, my grandmother from my mother's side of the family was my hero. She spoiled me with food and attention—you know how many grandparents love to spoil their grandchildren—and she always spoke on my behalf whenever I was in trouble. I spent a lot of time with my grandmother on her farm. My grandmother never wanted me to leave the village, and she always told me that if I went to school and learned, I would end up going crazy. She said that "learning too much book" would make a person crazy.

My grandmother had two daughters: my mother, who was named Kaikaiyah at birth, was the elder of her sister, Kebbeh. They were very close. Both sisters called their mother *Yeh*, which means "Mother" in the Kpelle language. I told everyone to call my grandmother *Yehloon*, which means "Small Mother," and to call my mother, *Yehketteh*, which means "Big Mother," because my mother was taller than her mother.

I also spent a lot of time with my grandfather from my father's side of the family. My grandfather was called Chief Kwalalon, and he was the chief of our village and the chief of several surrounding villages. Many times, he took me with him on trips to visit these other villages. My grandfather had built his own village outside of Yowee. His village was called Kpoloyei, which means "saltwater." The village was named after Kpoloyei River, but no one knows why the river is named this; maybe because it is sweet, or maybe because this is where people would come to purchase salt. Kpoloyei was also where everyone from Yowee fetched drinking water every day, even though it was over a mile away, because we did not have a well. It was a very important river and was located at one of the main approaches to Yowee. My grandfather was a very popular and powerful chief, and he had more than one wife. (I do not remember my grandmother from my father's side of the family, because she died when I was very young.) I have many fond memories of my grandfather.

In time, my older brother John was taken to Monrovia by my uncle, Samuel Faulkner, for the opportunity to receive an education. There was no school in our village, so to receive an education, we had to leave our village and go to Monrovia. I was very young when my older brother was taken away for school.

During those days, usually only boys were allowed by parents to go to school. Most girls were to stay in the village and learn how to be housewives. I believe this was one of the reasons my older sister, Yamah, stayed with my parents. Yamah was so nice to me. She was very helpful in taking care of me while our parents were out working, and she was trained at an early age to cook. She was very helpful to our mother.

Many of the indigenous Liberian people at this time did not understand the importance of an education. Very few could afford to send their children to school, as children often had to work on the farm to help support the family. Sometimes, indigenous parents would give their children to an Americo-Liberian family in order for them to be educated.

Most of the people in Yowee were farmers, but my father was not much involved in farming. He traveled often outside of our village to earn money. I still remember when he came home from one of his trips with a sewing machine (powered by pedaling his foot, as we had no electricity). He had learned how to sew, and he worked very hard to buy his own sewing machine. When he was able, he bought his first machine and brought it home and started sewing clothes for people. His tailoring skills earned him money and respect.

Through sewing, my father was able to support our family and travel much less. He used some of the money he earned from sewing to pay people to help farm for our family. He also was able to buy a sewing machine for his father-in-law, and it was through my father that my grandfather was able to learn how to sew and make money from sewing too. Through sewing, my father became very popular and famous and a hero to many people in our village and other villages surrounding us.

My father was the head of our household. I still remember when my father returned to Yowee from his trips; he always brought gifts for my mother, my sister, and me. These gifts might include toys or even a pet dog. These gifts were always very precious to us. My family was very poor, so we had few personal possessions. My father also brought special gifts for his father-in-law, such as a radio or a flashlight. Such items were not available to buy anywhere locally, and because of these gifts, my grandfather was vigorously supportive of my parents' relationship.

There were three important holidays that my father never missed coming home for. These holidays were Christmas, New Year's, and July 26, which is Liberia's Independence Day. No one ever celebrated birthdays, and Christmas, New Year's, and Independence Day were the only days for celebration and merry making. No one dared risk missing these celebrations.

For children, these were the only times we got new clothes. Growing up, I only ever had two sets of clothes at a time, but through my father's sewing, I always got Christmas clothes. He always tailored pants or shirts for me and my siblings from left over pieces of cloth.

Every parent worked so hard to make sure their children got new clothes and enough to eat on these holidays. However, many parents were indebted after the celebrations because they had to take out a loan in order for their families to take part.

And there was another special tradition in Liberia for these holidays. On these days, no family ever went to work on their farm.

Everybody stayed in town for the celebrations. There was traditional music and dance. Of course, most of the elders and older people of the village drank a lot of wine and other alcohol. It was a merry making day. Sometimes the villages would spend all week celebrating Christmas or the New Year.

During these celebrations, children spent a lot of time playing and enjoying their new clothes and toys, if parents were able to afford these things for them. Every quarter of the village had some party or dance or some event going on. I remember on one of these holidays, my father returned home from a short trip and brought me a jean jacket, a toy gun, and toy eyeglasses—wow! I was the best dressed guy that day; all my friends served me and honored me. I had received the best gifts, after all.

There was always food left over from these celebrations, and that was what we warmed over an open fire the next morning for a first meal. Most often, we only had enough food to eat one meal a day, so having two meals in one day was very special.

One of the most important and enjoyable parts of the Christmas and New Year's celebrations was that most of the young boys or men who had left the village for education in towns that had schools came home. There were no roads for cars to Yowee, so they had to walk to return to the village. Most of these boys came on Christmas Eve. They all met at Gbarnga, which was on the road system, and walked together to Yowee. Those in the village who had children in schools outside of the village always gathered at Kpoloyei River to see who was coming home.

In the early 1970s, telephones did not exist in the rural areas of Liberia, so no one knew who was coming home for the holidays. We never knew who would come until they showed up. My brother could never come home for Christmas because he could not afford the money it took. I did not see my brother for five years after my uncle took him to Monrovia. I was always disappointed not to see him when all the others came home for the celebrations.

One of the things I used to love as a boy was going to the farms with the older people. The reason was simple: there was food there. While my father spent most of his time sewing clothes for people when he was not traveling, my mother was busy singing in Yowee's farming coupe (co-op). A coupe is a group of farm owners that join together to work on each other's farms. For example, if a coupe is comprised of ten farmers, these ten farmers will go to one member's farm and work there for the whole day. They will do the same on each member's farm until all the work is done. This was the way when I was growing up and took place throughout the growing season, from planting to harvesting. The farm that hosted the coupe on a given day was always responsible to feed everyone.

Farming was and is still the way of life for those who live in Liberia's villages. Our way of farming is not the same as in developed nations. The people in Yowee only had manual tools, such as the machete, the axe, and the hoe. The routine is similar to holding a regular job in the United States, except it is farming. We got up every day and walked (roughly an hour) to the farm, worked all day, and returned home in the early evening to prepare dinner, wash clothes, and get ready for the next day. Children began working on the farms as soon as they were old enough.

My mother's job was to entertain the coupe by playing and singing traditional songs. She used an instrument called a *koino*, which is made out of bamboo. There were others who helped her, such as the drum beater and the vocal backers. The reason for the music was to keep the workers entertained so they could keep working. This process helped everyone to work harder and faster. It was amazing. One had to go by the beat of the music. In order for my mother to maintain her singing voice, she did not drink alcohol, but she did eat cola nuts, which grow on big trees and contain caffeine and have a bitter flavor.

Not only did my mother sing for the coupe, she also sang at church and taught my sister to sing. We attended a Lutheran church in my village, where my mother was the lead singer in the choir. She taught my sister to sing so she could replace her at the coupe or church if my mother got sick. I also learned my love of singing from my mother.

I miss my dear, sweet mother. She was a very important person to me, and no one can ever replace her. My mother was a good wife and a very good mother to me and my siblings—my father confirmed this many times whenever he sat me down to talk. She was very loving, caring, and hard working. It was my mother who encouraged me to be who I am today. She was very much involved in helping me make a decision to follow Christ, and she helped me decide on becoming a pastor, a man of God. She always reminded me to do good to people. She taught me that good character is better than silver or gold. And she taught me to always remember that there is a God.

My father, too, as head of our family, taught me many good things. He taught me about obedience, hard work, and honesty. He always told me to learn to work with my own hands. He taught me to give to others instead of always wanting to receive. My parents were both exemplary community members and parents. Even though I did not spend all of my childhood with my parents, the short period I did spend with them was very formative and a blessing.

When I was seven, my father sent me to live with my aunty. My father wanted me to learn how to read and write, and my aunty's husband was the principal of a school and also a teacher. Teachers were highly respected and honored in our village society. Though she was concerned about my well-being, my mother agreed to this arrangement. My parents thought I was going to be allowed to attend school, but they were wrong, very wrong.

According to my father, his father did not want me to leave the village and go to school. So when my father made the decision to send me away, he did not tell my grandfather. My grandmother told me to run away if my aunty came to take me.

But in the end, I went to live with my aunty far away in her village of Gborta. To get to Gborta, my aunty and I had to walk over three hours through the jungle from Yowee to a city called Foequelleh, which was located along a road that cars could travel. Then we had to catch a taxi about fifty miles from Foequelleh to Gborta. Gborta was much bigger than Yowee, and at the time, it had an elementary school, where my aunty's husband was the principal.

When I came to live in Gborta, instead of sending me to school, my aunty and her husband sent me to work on their farm. At first I enjoyed going to the farm, because it was similar to the work I did in Yowee. At school, I knew, I would have to speak English, but I did not know how to speak English or how to read and write, and on the farm, everyone spoke Kpelle. We planted rice during the rice season, and we planted other crops, such as cassava and plantains, and a hot pepper garden.

Liberia is comprised of sixteen tribal people, and they speak the tribal languages of their villages. I was born into the Kpelle tribe (the largest of the sixteen tribes) and only spoke Kpelle. The indigenous Liberian tribes (the Kpelle, Bassa, Gio, Kru, Grebo, Mano, Krahn, Gola, Gbandi, Lorma, Kissi, Vai, Dei, Bella, Mandingo, and Mende) account for 95 percent of the population of Liberia. Americo-Liberians make up another 2.5 percent, and Congo people (descendants of immigrants from the Caribbean who had been slaves) make up the other 2.5 percent. It was very common for a child not to be able to speak English.

I was comfortable on the farm at first. However, the work I could not do for my parents because I was so young was just what I was forced to do for my aunty and her husband. My aunty had two children from a prior relationship who were older than me, and these children worked on the farm also. Only the children fathered by my aunty's husband were allowed to go to school and did not have to work on the farm.

It was an unfortunate situation, and there was nothing I could do to change it. I was very far from my parents, and there was little means of communication at this time. Unless someone was traveling to another village, we could not send or receive a message—no email or telephones—and the primary means of travel was a human being walking the distance from one place to another. I had no way to tell my parents what I was going through.

Working on the farm became very difficult for a young boy. I had to get up early in the morning, between four and five o'clock, to start walking to the farm. It took me between two and three hours to walk to the farm, just one way, and I had to start work as soon as I arrived. If my aunty was told by anyone that I did not make it on time, I was in big trouble. I would get a real flogging from my aunty or her husband, and sometimes the both of them would flog me together. They would beat me with whatever they had—a switch, a branch, a broom.

We usually worked seven days a week. I remember only sometimes not working on New Year's Eve, the only day of the year my aunty went to church. Though, sometimes I was able to play soccer with her two older children. We also were allowed to go hunting if our work was done.

Miracles do happen. I don't know how my mother got word that my aunty and her husband were not sending me to school, but I believe it was a miracle from God. One evening while returning from the farm, I met someone on the way who told me that my mother had come to get me. I was so happy to hear the news, and I hurried into town to see if it was true. When my mother saw me, she hugged me and cried. My mother told me that night that she had come to take me home. What she wanted me to do was to cry and tell my aunty that I was going with my mother. But the next morning, I was threatened by my aunty that if I cried to go with my mother, I was going to pay a price that I was never going to forget my entire lifetime.

In the presence of my mother, my aunty pretended she really loved and cared for me. My mother knew that she was pretending, so my mother insisted that I should say to my aunty that I wanted to go with her. But my aunty had already threatened to flog me if I said that my mother should take me with her. What could I do? I really wanted to go with my mother, but I was terrified of my aunty. She was never going to allow my mother to take me.

On the day that my mother was leaving for her village, she told me to insist that I was going with her, and I wanted to insist. My aunty realized that I wanted to go with mother, so she told me to leave their presence, but my mother said no. There was arguing between my aunty and my mother. Many bystanders arrived to try to settle the matter, but my aunty was very powerful in Gborta.

My poor mother was very upset about my aunty's demand that I continue to live with her. My aunty insisted that my mother did not have power over me because I was her brother's son and that it was my aunty's brother, my father, who had the final say, not my mother. In those days in Liberia, a mother did not have a lot of power over her children. In this case, my father was not present to say who should take me, so some of Gborta's elders came and appealed to my mother to leave me with my aunty and go talk with my father, because he had given me to his sister. I was forced by my aunty to say to my mother that I was not going with her and instead wanted to stay with my aunty.

My aunty won the battle, and my poor mother left in tears. After my mother's departure, my aunty called me and told me that my mother had no power over me but she, my aunty, did. I was punished because I had told my aunty I wanted to go with my mother. The punishment was very harsh. I was not allowed to eat for the whole day, and I had to do 150 squats. I was asked to count from 1 to 150. Remember, I did not know how to read or write, or count. Because I could not count to 150, I was asked to start counting all over again many times. My legs were like rubber. That day is one of the many days I have never forgotten.

Because I was not able to count out the 150 squats, I was flogged so much that I could not cry or walk, but I was forced to walk, which caused me to fall down. I dropped on the ground outside my aunty's house for a long period of time. During this time, my aunty pretended that she was not afraid of what any neighbor thought. But there was a God-sent man who saw me and picked me up and took me to the river and bathed me, and after he fed me some rice, I laid down and quickly fell asleep. After I woke, the man took me back to my aunty and appealed that she forgive me and not beat me like that again. Praise God for that man. Unfortunately, I cannot remember who he was.

This man pled for me even though he was afraid of my aunty. My aunty's husband was a teacher and was considered very powerful, so everyone was afraid of him and his household. But, although I was a part of that household, I was not his child. There were so many differences between the treatment of his biological children and me. His children ate better, were dressed in nice clothes, and attended school. I ate what food was available, had only two sets of clothes, and I had to work on the farm all day. I was still only eight years old.

This life became normal to me. While living with my aunty, I never realized what love was because I was never loved by my aunty or her husband. Even their children treated me like an animal. I could never complain because I was always in the wrong, no matter what. Every time I took a complaint to my aunty, she would tell me to get out of her face. I grew up for a long time without love.

Since I have come to know the Lord Jesus Christ, I have been able to forgive my aunty and her husband for all the abuse they committed against me.

2 ~ GOING HOME

I learned a lot from the mistreatment and hardship I suffered when I lived with my aunty. I learned that life is not always as easy for an eight-year-old child as one would think. At this time in my life, I had to do whatever I was told to do, whether I liked it or not, or whether I could do it or not. I just had to do as best I could. And if my tasks were not done correctly, I would be flogged until I learned to do them right. These were not short floggings, and they were very painful.

I learned discipline, how to be strong, how to face the challenges of life, and how to survive in difficult situations. I also learned to help others, because there were many people I did not know who came to my aid during this difficult time. These people taught me how to stand up for people who are suffering. God wants us to always look out for the helpless and needy, and when we stand up for the helpless and the needy, we help push them forward in life. I have learned that God has a plan for everyone, and no matter what condition we are facing now, we can look through the suffering and see God at work in our lives. The lessons I learned while living with my aunty would benefit me greatly during the long years of war later in my life.

These circumstances continued for me for about four years until one day, when I was about twelve, another boy was sent to live with my aunty. I still remember his English name, Moses. Moses was about eighteen years old. Through Moses, I gained my deliverance from Egypt. As God sent Moses back to Egypt to free His people, my Moses was sent to show me the way out of my Egypt and away from my aunty and her husband, my Egyptian masters. I wish I could find Moses today and thank him.

Like me, Moses was sent to live with my aunty and her husband so he could receive education, but as they treated me, so they treated him. Instead of being sent to school, Moses was sent to work on the farm also. However, my aunty and her husband could not flog or punish Moses as harshly as they did me. The village Moses came from (I forget the name) was much closer to Gborta, and his parents might have heard he was not being treated well. Moses was also a bigger boy than me, and he could fight back. He could always say no to any punishment that he didn't want to receive.

Moses saw my poor condition and felt very sorry for me. One day while Moses and I were on the farm working, he told me he had a plan and he wanted to know what I thought. He told me he could only reveal his plan to me if I could promise not to tell anyone. That day Moses did not reveal his plan, because he did not trust that I could keep it to myself. But the next day I asked Moses about the plan. He asked me, "Do you really want me to tell you?" I said yes. Moses made me vow I would not tell anyone, and if I did tell anyone, he said he would never again trust me or care for me. I promised not to tell anyone.

Moses told me he had decided to leave Gborta and go back to his parents' village, because the reality of coming to stay with my aunty and her husband was not what he and his parents had expected, and he also wanted to help me get back to my village. My question to Moses was how we could go about this plan, because the distance to my village, Yowee, was so far away. He told me that he was going to help me find a way to escape but I would need transportation in order to return home.

Every Wednesday in Gborta was set aside as a market day. This meant that people from other villages would bring their food products to Gborta on Wednesday to sell to people from larger towns or the city, and people from larger towns or the city would bring goods to sell to the villagers. Vendors from the city would bring things such as salt, clothes, shoes, radios, flashlights, and batteries, and the villagers would bring palm oil, bananas, plantains, and many other local foodstuffs.

Wednesdays were good for me, because they were days I was allowed to stay in town and sell dried fish or bread. I got to see all the different products that people brought in from their farms to sell, and I met a lot of people. I was always hoping to see someone from Yowee or someone who knew my parents. I wished that every day could be a Wednesday.

It was on one of these Wednesdays that we attempted Moses's

plan to escape. The first thing Moses did was to find the way to Yowee from Gborta, because I did not remember. He found someone who was able to give him directions to Yowee by way of Foequelleh—which, remember, was the nearest town to Yowee by car—but we would need one dollar to pay for transportation from Gborta to Foequelleh. There were two potential problems I saw with this plan: I did not know the way to Yowee from Foequelleh, so I did not know how I would make it all the way home, and Moses would not be coming with me; I would have to make this long journey all by myself. This all seemed too difficult for me.

The only means of getting the one dollar we needed for my transportation to Foequelleh was to steal it from the money we made selling fish. I was very afraid to do this, because I knew the harsh penalty I would pay if I was caught. But Moses said it was the only way the plan was going to work. I finally agreed to take the money, but instead of taking the full dollar, I only took seventy-five cents.

Later that day, the man who had given Moses directions to Foequelleh took him to a driver who traveled to Foequelleh often. This man was from the Mandingo tribe and a Muslim. He knew Foequelleh well and knew people who knew of Yowee. The blessed thing about this Wednesday was it was also a market day in Foequelleh. This meant it would be very possible to find someone from Yowee there selling their crops.

Moses came and found me and told me he had found someone who was willing to take me to Foequelleh. He told me that I had to leave right away, but I still had the balance of the fish and the rest of the money from my sales that day. I hurriedly took the money and the balance of the fish to my aunty's house—she was not there. I placed the money on her table in her room and placed the dried fish beside the money and left to meet Moses and the driver. When I reached them, the driver asked us for the dollar, but I had only taken seventy-five cents. The driver said if I could not pay the full dollar, then he would put me in the trunk of his car and I would pay fifty cents.

Moses told me to say yes because this was our only chance of success. So I paid the fifty cents and was put in the trunk of the car with a goat—I saved the remaining twenty-five cents to purchase something to eat on my journey. Moses stood waiting for the car to leave before he, too, headed back to his parents' village, on foot. I was in the trunk of the car with the goat, holding the trunk lid open with one hand and waving goodbye to Moses with the other. He was waving to me with a big smile. This is how I fled Egypt, away from my aunty and her husband. Freedom at last.

God has a plan for every one of us. He will always make a way for the poor and innocent. Even though I didn't know God then, He certainly knew me and loved me, in spite of my condition. He made a way for me. The driver and I arrived in Foequelleh late in the afternoon and headed for the market to find someone who might be going to Yowee, and the first few people we asked told us yes, there were many people from Yowee who had come to the market but many had already left for home. I was so afraid. The driver and I were still asking around when an old lady told us that there was still one family headed toward Yowee that was waiting for their father. He had gone to drink wine with some friends at the palm wine camp nearby. The old lady told us to go to the junction of the trail to Yowee and there we would find the family.

The driver and I hurried to the junction and indeed found the family. God is so good. I believe God placed that family there to wait for me. When the driver and I reached them, he asked if they were going to Yowee. They said they were, but they were waiting for their father. Because the driver had to go, he asked the people to kindly allow me to walk with them on the way to Yowee then left. Soon, the father returned from the palm wine camp, and his family spoke to him about my situation.

The father asked for my name. When I gave it, he became very happy and hugged me and told me he knew me when I was in Yowee, but he was confusing me with my older brother, John. I was a little afraid, because the father smelled of palm wine and I thought he was drunk, but he gave my parents' names and told me that he was my father-in-law. I came to understand that my parents had engaged John to the man's niece when they were younger. See how God works? He had prepared these people to stay behind just for my sake. God really is good. I cannot remember the name of this family, but I am indebted to them for returning me to my home and my family.

The father asked me, "Where is your load?" meaning baggage. I had nothing, and I told him so. He said, "You come from that big town, and you don't have anything with you?" I replied yes. He asked me again where my clothes were, and I replied that I didn't have any clothes. He asked me what was wrong, and I told him my story. Then he told me he was going to take me to my parents, but first we were going to stop at his farm so we could eat and rest awhile before leaving for Yowee.

We all went to the family's farm, and my brother's fiancé cooked our meal that evening. This was the first time in many years I had eaten so much and had food left over—I really ate a lot that afternoon. After eating, everybody went to the river and took a bath. I had no fresh clothes, so afterward, I put back on the clothes I had been wearing for more than two weeks. They were very dirty and smelled, but it meant nothing to me, and I believe it didn't matter to the family either.

We left the family's farm late that evening and arrived at Yowee after walking for several hours in the dark. My parents had also returned from their farm. My father had gone to speak to his in-laws, and my mother had just come back from getting drinking water from the river. My mother had a bucket of water on her head and was holding another in her hand. I was just walking toward my parents' house with the man who brought me home when my mother saw me and quickly put down her buckets of water and ran toward me. I was so happy to see my mother, and she was crying tears of joy.

I felt that my life could begin again. I was home under the protection of my mother and family. I had peace.

Liberia was also experiencing peace at this time.

3 ~ LIFE IN MONROVIA

The news about my return to Yowee spread so quickly and so wide that many of my relatives came from outside the village to see if it was true. I believe the year I fled from my aunty and her husband was 1976, around June or July. The reason I believe this is I finally celebrated Independence Day that year in my home village after roughly five years. Many of my relatives became very angry with my father for allowing his sister to treat me so wrongly. My mother, too, was very angry with my father for sending me to live with his sister, and she argued with my father that whole night.

I remember my grandmother telling my father she had told him long before she didn't want my aunty to take me away, but my father had refused to listen and sent me to live with her anyway. My grandmother told my father that his sister was a wicked woman. My father told my mother and grandmother to wait and see if his sister would come to Yowee to look for me. He promised to find out his sister's side of the story. But my aunty did not care; she didn't even send a message to my parents to find out if I was safe. I did not see her again until 2004, when my father died.

The year I returned to Yowee, the Christmas and New Year's celebrations were memorable for me because I, too, was able to put on a happy face at the river when I saw that my brother was among those who had returned for the holidays. I did not recognize my brother at first, but once I did, I was very happy to see him after so many years. He was surprised to see me too. Mom was the first to tell my brother about my problems. He became very upset hearing about the way our aunty had treated me. He decided he was going to take me with him to Monrovia, even though he was struggling there. He said he would ask another extended family member, another aunty, to take care of me.

Going with my brother to Monrovia involved the risk that he would not be able to find anyone interested in taking me in. The result of which could mean I would be sent back to the village or I would end up on the street. My brother was afraid to take me to live with him with our Uncle Faulkner, because there was no space for me. My brother also had not informed our uncle I would be coming.

We traveled from Yowee to Monrovia with other boys and young men, all of whom lived with relatives or other sponsors in Monrovia in order to go to school. All of these boys and young men changed their native names when they came to Monrovia, often to the name of the family they lived with. Very few kept their native given or family names. John was not my brother's native name, for example. John's native name had been Gorlon, which is the name of a small bird in Liberia, but when he moved to Monrovia to go to school, he took John.

We arrived in Monrovia late at night, and the city was different than anywhere I had lived before. There were more cars, streets, and tall buildings, and almost everybody spoke English. The next morning, my brother took me to one of our distant aunties. My brother explained my story to her and appealed to her to take me in.

This aunty's name was Edna, and we were not biologically related. Her uncle was a friend of our Uncle Faulkner, and she was also from the Kpelle tribe, and it is common in Liberia to consider ourselves relatives in these circumstances. Aunty Edna was married and had one son from an earlier relationship who was only home occasionally to spend time with his mother. Edna and her husband lived in one rented room, and she agreed to let me live with them, but because it was only one room, I had to sleep on a mat on the floor. Aunty Edna and her husband slept on the bed. This was early in the year 1977, and I was thirteen years old.

I stayed with Aunty Edna from 1977 to 1978. During this time, I would work for her selling bread and fried fish in the morning and go to school in the evening, and after school, I was expected to go out and sell the balance of the bread and fish from the morning. I also did the dish washing and cleaning of the room and yard. The school I attended was Richard M. Nixon Elementary, named after President Nixon of the United States.

As a young boy, I loved to play soccer and other games with my friends, but Aunty Edna did not like the idea of me having fun with other boys. All she wanted me to do was keep busy by working all day long. But as a boy, I needed time to play, especially soccer. So, many times after school, when she was still at work, I would go and play with my friends. Whenever she found out, she would punish me. But these punishments were never as harsh as the punishments of my first aunty. Aunty Edna, for example, would punish me by not allowing me to play soccer. However, because I loved soccer so much, this punishment was terrible enough.

One day after school had closed for summer vacation, my Aunty Edna told my brother that she could not keep me because I was too hardheaded. John begged our aunty to allow me to stay, but she refused. What could he do? He was already sharing a small room with four other people, and they did not want a little boy staying there. John pleaded with his four roommates to allow me to sleep in his spot on the floor and he would find somewhere else to sleep, but they refused. He was very worried.

When Aunty Edna finally decided to give up on me, I was surprised and confused. I felt hurt. I always did my work before playing. I did very well selling bread and fish for her. I was always up by five in the morning, mixing flour for the bread or cleaning fish. I also helped to cook the evening meal, usually consisting of rice and a soup made from cassava leaves, beans, and chicken or fish. Why was she doing this to me?

Aunty Edna told my brother that if he needed help for me, she would still try to help out in small ways. But I said within myself that I was never going to ask for anything from her again. If this meant I died, I was willing to die. I even refused the leftover bread and fish she offered me. I wanted to prove to my aunty that I could survive without her. After she turned me over to my brother, he asked me what we were going to do about the situation. I told John that I was going to try to find my way by myself. I told him that I would find my own place to sleep and my own way to live.

"How?" John asked me—I was still only thirteen years old.

"You will see," I told him.

Life started all over for me, again. I was in Monrovia with nowhere to start from and nowhere to go. My poor brother was very worried about what to do. He wanted to help, but he didn't have the means, as he himself was struggling. John had been trying to attend night school, but it was very hard for him because he was apprenticing under a mechanic who was teaching him how to repair cars. He went to this man every morning and came home around five thirty or six in the evening. Then he needed to find something to eat before getting ready for school. It was so hard that John had to drop out of school, particularly when our Uncle Faulkner was not able pay his school fees. John quit school in the ninth grade.

Despite his struggles, every day John finished job training, he tried to find some food for both of us. Sometimes he would give me all of the little food he found, while he went to bed hungry. He would ask people about me, and when he was told where I was, he would come find me to see how I was doing. I could see the stress I caused him. I was his little brother whom he had brought from the village to the city, and he felt responsible for me.

I knew a little bit about selling and knew my way around Monrovia from when I sold bread and fried fish for my Aunty Edna. But I did not know where I could find money to start my own business. Eventually, I started working for my friend, Isaac, shining shoes in the Buzzie Quarter on United Nations Drive, very close to Liberia's Executive Mansion, which is Liberia's White House. The neighborhood was called the Buzzie Quarter, because many of its residents were from the Lorma tribe, and Buzzie is another name for a Lorma tribe member. The Lorma tribe is from Lofa County, one of the largest counties in Liberia.

Every morning starting around six thirty, I would go and help Isaac shine shoes, and he would pay me out of the amount I earned that day. School was closed for Christmas vacation at that time, so I was working in order to raise money for the next school year. I already had my old uniform from the past school year, so I needed to earn just enough money for notebooks, shoes, pencils, and registration fees. The first day I worked for Isaac, he paid me a dollar, and I got fifty cents more from a man whose shoes I shined. This man told me I was his friend and he wanted me to always be the one to shine his shoes.

In those days, government schools were not too expensive. Around twenty to twenty-five dollars could take me through a semester. It was usual for government school teachers to sometimes request extra money from students for things such as taking a makeup exam or as a bribe to pass their class. However, the greatest requirement at that time was the school uniform. All government school children were required to wear a uniform.

A uniform cost between twelve and fifteen dollars, and this was a lot of money for someone like me. Even many parents could not afford the cost of uniforms for their children. The color of the uniform depended on the school, and the uniform for Richard M. Nixon Elementary was a yellow shirt, blue trousers, black shoes, and white socks. I was not allowed in school unless I wore my uniform.

There were many of us shoe-shine boys in the Buzzie Quarter, but Isaac became my best friend. This didn't happen until I stood up to him in a fight. In order to make it among the shoe-shine boys, I had to be strong; otherwise, they would have taken advantage of me. Many of the city boys thought because I was from the villages I was lazy, but they were wrong, very wrong.

The first day Isaac and I fought, I was afraid of him, so he was able to knock me down. At that fight, there were many boys standing around. No one was allowed to part us or stop us from fighting. Everybody stood aside to watch us fight. After that first fight, one of the other boys told me not to be afraid of Isaac. He said to me, "Man, you can beat that guy if you stop being afraid." He said this was no-man's-land, that only the strong could survive. That day I was encouraged and decided that I was going to stand up to Isaac if he tried to fight me again.

The next morning, we went to start work as usual. We had to get up early in the morning to find a good spot to shine shoes. If we found a good spot but were lazy, someone who was stronger could take it. I was already used to getting up early because of village life, and that morning I got up early and found two spots: one for the boy who told me not to be afraid to fight Isaac and one for myself. When Isaac arrived, he demanded that I give him my spot. I refused, so once again, we got into a fight. This time, I was able to show everyone I was not someone that anyone could just knock down easily. I beat Isaac that morning, and he could not believe it.

It was from this fight that Isaac and I became good friends. After that day, I became part of the group. I also became more confident. I was strong, and I could face anyone who attempted to fight me. To be able to survive, I had to be strong. Life at this time was a struggle for me, but I was very serious about going to school, and this gave me focus.

The amount I earned from shining shoes for a day depended on the number of shoes I shined. Some days were good and some days were not good. On a not good day, I made just enough for food (about fifty cents to one dollar) or I would have to borrow money from one of my friends. We could always ask one another for a loan, though sometimes the lender would require interest. During that Christmas vacation working for Isaac, I was able to save fifty dollars to pay for a year of school. All of the money I earned went to John for safe keeping. Every evening I would go to see him and would give him whatever I had earned that day. I became a great help to my brother.

During this time, I didn't have anywhere to sleep, so I slept in a taxi driver's taxi. I would wash it every morning in exchange for being allowed to sleep there. The parking lot where the taxi was parked had security, but if a driver wanted to allow someone to sleep in his car, he could. This was my first sleeping place after I left my Aunty Edna's. There were other boys who slept in other cars in the lot too, so I was not the only one who did this.

My brother wanted to know where I slept, but I lied to him and told him that I had a good place to sleep. One day he came early from job training to see where I was really sleeping. I took him to a lady I knew from the Buzzie Quarter and said that I slept at her house with her sons. I told this lady not to tell my brother the truth. This lady was very nice to me. Sometimes she saved food for me, and I kept my few clothes at her house. I sometimes drew water for her and washed her children's clothes. Every time my brother came to her house to find me, she would tell him that she had sent me somewhere. This lady took care of my uniform and my notebooks, and I got myself a book bag to carry all of my notebooks in. Before school reopened, I was ready.

When my brother brought me to Monrovia it was 1977. I stayed with my Aunty Edna for one year while I was in first grade. By the end of the 1977 school year, Aunty Edna said she could not keep me. So I started living on my own in 1978, and started putting myself through school. When I was fourteen, I was promoted to the second grade at Richard M. Nixon Elementary, and I was still living on my own. And I continued on my own until the time God called me to follow Him.

By the Grace of God, I kept my focus on school, and this helped me survive. In the morning from about six thirty to noon, I shined shoes. From one in the afternoon to five in the evening, I went to school. It was a rough year, but God brought me through it. I was blessed to have two good friends, also from the Kpelle tribe but from different villages. We spoke Kpelle together, which was a great comfort to me, and we were in the same class at school. One of these friends was named James Winnie, and I still see him when I am in Liberia. My other friend's name was Daniel, but I cannot remember his last name.

James and Daniel had been sent to live with a lady from Ghana so they could attend school in Monrovia. She would make corn bread and short bread and give it to James and Daniel to sell at the St. Theresa Convent School, which was a Catholic all-girls school. She rented a space in the school cafeteria for them to sell her bread while she went to work.

At this time, I switched from shining shoes to selling boiled eggs. Selling eggs was a much cleaner job than shining shoes. I would purchase raw eggs from a store and boil them at the home of the kind lady in the Buzzie Quarter. I would then sell the boiled eggs alongside James and Daniel's bread. However, if the lady from Ghana had found out that I was using her space and not paying rent, there would have been serious trouble for James and Daniel, so every time this lady came to the school to check on James and Daniel, I would have to hide.

At the end of the 1978 school year, I decided to change to a school closer to where I was living in the Buzzie Quarter. The name of my new school was Lorma Quarter Elementary School. It was built by a governor from the Lorma tribe, Kezzel Kollie. Even though I changed schools, I still maintained my friendships with James and Daniel, but I started selling eggs in other places. Often, we would spend time together where they lived with the lady from Ghana when she was not there.

While enrolled at Lorma Quarter Elementary School, I continued to support myself by selling boiled eggs, and I started shining shoes again. Third grade was a difficult school year for me because I had to work so much. I went from being an A student to a C student. However, I did have a teacher who became like a second mother to me, Mrs. Tulay. Mrs. Tulay was from the Lorma tribe, which is the closest tribe to the Kpelle. The Kpelle tribe is considered the uncle of the Lorma tribe, and both tribes have much in common.

That year, I had to attend summer school because I had failed one major class, but after finishing the summer term, I was promoted to fourth grade. This was in 1979. Fourth grade was not as difficult a year. My teacher's name was Mrs. Tucker, and she was Kpelle, like me. I owe her a lot of gratitude. Many times, she would come out onto the streets to find me and take me to class. She remained involved in my life through the rest of my education at Lorma Quarter Elementary.

I owe both of these teachers my life. I live out the legacy they gave me. They were God-sent.

I believe that living with my first aunty prepared me mentally and physically for my early years in Monrovia. Living in the city is much harder than living in the villages when it comes to finding food and a place to sleep. In the villages, you can find food by going into the bush or to a farm. You can also sleep on a farm whether or not the owners are present. If the farm owners are present, you just ask them if you can spend the night, and they will let you and share a meal with you. This is the Liberian way.

City life is very different and very difficult compared with the villages. Almost all my bad habits came from living in the city, and if I had the power, no one would ever experience the neglect, abuse, hunger, stress, or fear that I lived through as a child. However, my past difficulties have helped me become the man I am today. I am able to support and encourage others because of all the bad situations that I went through in my early life, and these experiences helped me learn to be a survivor.

When I was fifteen years old, I had been living on my own for two years. Liberia was at peace, but even though everything appeared calm, there were many realities that indigenous Liberians did not care for. The Americo-Liberians were in control, and they had all of the privileges and power. Previously, indigenous Liberians did not know a lot about politics, but this was starting to change.

Many indigenous Liberians were in the army, and most had no education, so they did not think they had any other option except to follow the commands of their leaders. They did what they were told to do without complaining.

However, around 1978, many other indigenous Liberians like me were being educated, and because of their education, they started speaking out. Many indigenous Liberians attended the University of Liberia in Monrovia and were involved in the student union there. It was in part through the University of Liberia

Student Union that the rice riot of April 1979 happened. The foundation for the Liberian Civil War was about to be laid.

In 1979, President Tolbert and his agricultural ministry decided to increase the price of rice, the staple food in Liberia, from twenty-two dollars to thirty dollars per one-hundred-pound bag. This eight-dollar increase represented more than one-third of the average monthly income for a Liberian. Tolbert's family was the dominant importer of rice to Liberia.

Indigenous leaders told Tolbert raising the price of rice was not fair to the poor, who were already suffering. Tolbert did not listen to the cry of the people and decided to go ahead with the price increase. Amos Sawyer, a professor at the University of Liberia, Baccus Matthews, and Togbah Nah Tipoteh, among others, were leaders and heroes at this time for indigenous Liberians. They spoke for the masses. Our indigenous heroes rallied the people to demonstrate against Tolbert and the price increase.

On April 14, 1979, about twelve thousand native sons and daughters took to the streets of Monrovia in protest against Tolbert. Some friends and I joined the demonstration. I was shining shoes with my friends, and when the crowd of demonstrators came close, we put our shoe-shine boxes away and joined the crowd. We were heading to the Rally Town Market area of Monrovia, which is close to Buzzie Quarter, where I lived, and to the Barclay Training Center, where the Liberian Army barracks is located.

The President had told the police director to tell the people that the Liberian National Police were under orders to shoot and kill anyone found in the streets demonstrating. The Liberian National Police confronted the crowd and asked everyone to leave, which we refused to do. One police officer took out his gun and shot and wounded one of the demonstrators, and another man was beaten by the police. Some men in the crowd took the man who had been shot and held him in the air for all to see.

Because the crowd continued to refuse to disperse, the police opened fire and killed at least forty people (some reports state this number was in the hundreds). Tolbert, an Americo-Liberian, ordered the army, which was composed mostly of indigenous Liberians, to support the outnumbered police officers and fire on the crowd. But the army refused and instead defended the demonstrators, so the police fled.

Then the army started looting local businesses, and this went on throughout the night. Many innocent civilians were killed, but by the grace of God, I was not harmed. John came looking for me and took me with him to where he was staying at the time, because it was very dangerous to be where I lived in the Buzzie Quarter. The leaders of the demonstrations were all arrested and put into jail, and they were not freed until after President Tolbert was killed in Samuel Doe's coup on April 12, 1980.

April 14, 1979, was the first major spilling of blood in Monrovia. The next day, everyone was warned not to go into the streets, so I stayed with my brother all day.

After a few days, things returned to normal, and I started my daily struggle again.

4 ~ DOE TAKES OVER

When I first came to Monrovia, my uncle named me Wilmon Faulkner, but the name was too hard for me to pronounce and spell. I was not living with my Uncle Faulkner at the time, like John, so I changed my name to George Sackie. Later as a young man, I decided to take my father's name, Sackie, as my first name and my grandfather's name, Kwalalon, as my last name. The reason I did this was to carry on our grandfather's name, because none of my brothers, sisters, or cousins had my grandfather's name as their last name. Even my uncle did not use our grandfather's name, so I felt our grandfather was being cheated. It is very important in Liberian culture to carry on family names, and I was living on my own, so I felt I could do as I wanted.

After a year of street life in Monrovia, I was invited to live at my Uncle Faulkner's house by his son, my cousin, Wilfred. Wilfred lived in Uncle Faulkner's house with his parents and his half-sister, Jatu, and his half-brother, Mbangda, whom his father had had with another woman. At first, Wilfred did not tell his parents that he had brought me to live with them; he took me in on his own. He did this because he saw that I needed help but did not want to go through the formality of talking to his parents.

Wilfred was much younger than I was, but because he provided me a place to live, I lived under his control. I knew he had the power to throw me out because he was a son and I was only a cousin. If he thought I cheated him in gambling, he would toss me out. Or if I beat him in soccer, he might toss me out. Sometimes he would simply tell me to leave his room for no particular reason and later say he was sorry and call me back. I think this was part of being young men; we had misunderstandings all the time. I finally went to complain to Uncle Faulkner, but he only told me it was his son who brought me into the house and not himself, so his son had the right to throw me out or bring me in again. I decided to go back to the streets instead of trying to talk things out with Wilfred.

After I left my uncle's house, a man named Big Boy took me in. Big Boy was about twenty-eight years old and provided a refuge for many of us who didn't have a regular place to sleep. His room was very small—about six by six feet. There was one old and spoiled bed with no mattress. We used cardboard as mattresses. More than ten boys lived with Big Boy in that one little room, and there was barely any space to sleep. I was still in school at this time. Only the strong could survive, and I had to survive.

Big Boy was very strong. We all looked to him for protection; we faced much danger on the streets from older boys and other men. He was like a big brother to me. Also during this time, Big Boy's grandmother grew to love me. She used to sell palm oil and dried meat at the Rally Town Market close to the Buzzie Quarter. Palm oil is an edible oil derived from the pulp of the fruit of the palm tree. It is a very common cooking oil in Liberia, because it is inexpensive and readily available. Big Boy's grandma would ask me to come visit her in the market on my way from school.

Big Boy's grandmother came to love me because, one Sunday, she asked Big Boy to bring some of his boys to help raise the ground at a spot where she wanted to build a small house. This spot was next to a river, and when the river overflowed its bank, it would flood the area, so we needed to raise the level of ground where the house would be built. A few of us went to help Grandma. I worked so hard that day, and she was so happy with me that she told me I was now her grandson. I told her I would work on her house every following Sunday until it was built, and I did.

Big Boy's grandmother reminded me of my own grandmother back in Yowee. I still remember one Christmas vacation when I returned with John to Yowee for the Christmas and New Year's celebrations. When my grandma saw me, she asked me how much book I knew by then; she asked me what grade I was in. I said that I was in the second grade, and she said that if I passed to the third grade, I should stop before I went crazy. The next year when I went home again, I told her that I was still in the second grade, but I was lying. If I had told her I was promoted to the third grade, she would have said to stop there. The year I was promoted to ninth grade, 1985, when I was twenty-one years old, Grandma went to be with the Lord.

When my grandmother was living, she was always concerned about me. Every time Grandma heard someone was going to Monrovia, she would cook food for me and wrap the food in leaves and send it with that person to give to me. The food never made it. The person always ate the food on the way. To travel from Yowee to Monrovia at that time took two or three days. A person would have to walk from our village to a town that had a road for cars. If he got to the town late, he might have to sleep there because of the lack of cars going to Gbarnga, and from Gbarnga to Monrovia, which was about a half day's drive. How could someone travel with cooked food for such a distance and not eat it?

And Big Boy's grandmother reminded me of my own grandmother. She was so kind to me. Many times, I went to see her in the evening when she came home from the market. I don't know what happened, but one day I was told that Big Boy's grandmother was leaving for Lofa County, over two hundred miles away, where her children lived. One of the kindest women I have known left my life.

Things changed for me again. No one was there to show me love and care. But no matter how hard things got for me, I kept my focus on going to school. My parents could not afford to pay for my education, and my mother wanted me to return to the village, but this would have meant failure for me. Remember, I had said in my heart that I was going to make it on my own, because of my second aunty giving up on me. Returning to Yowee would have felt like failure, so I refused to go back there. At this time, John was working in Kakata, thirty-five miles outside Monrovia, and not around to help me either. So there I was.

Things were also changing for Liberia.

Samuel Kanyon Doe, a member of the Krahn tribe, joined the Liberian Army in 1969. He was born in Tuzon in southeastern Liberia. This area of Liberia is thickly forested and thinly populated. The Krahn tribe is one of the smallest tribes in Liberia, comprising about 5 percent of the population and, at the time, were mostly uneducated. Doe's father was a private in the Liberia Armed Forces. Doe's wife, Nancy, was a seller of wares on the streets just outside the Rally Time Market in Monrovia.

Samuel Doe became a master sergeant and, on April 12, 1980, he led a bloody coup against the elected president of Liberia, William Tolbert. Doe, along with seventeen of his men, murdered

Tolbert and twenty-six of his supporters, who were mostly America-Liberian, and then set up a military regime. Doe called himself a "type of Christ" because he was the first indigenous ruler of Liberia; he was from the people and not from the America-Liberian ruling class.

In the weeks following the coup, America-Liberians had their properties seized. Many more were killed, and many fled the country. Liberia was soon under the control of Doe's People's Redemption Council, and it soon became apparent the regime had no idea how to run a country. They were without training, education, or experience.

In the beginning, however, though many Liberians were shocked to hear of the coup, many people supported Doe. The people in Monrovia celebrated in the streets because they thought Doe would allow more access to education, business, and government for the indigenous people of Liberia. The new leaders made it known that the era of America-Liberian domination was over and now the indigenous Liberians were in control.

The new leaders promised justice and equality for all. But then the constitution was suspended and martial law declared. All political activities were banned. State sanctioned violence and murders became commonplace as Doe consolidated his power by killing anyone who opposed his rule. And it was not long before Liberians realized that the country was heading toward total chaos.

Normally in a military coup, the military command structure takes the place of civilian authority. But in Liberia, the military command structure was mostly made up of America-Liberians, and the PRC arrested and killed most of them, leaving a vacuum of leadership. The PRC learned quickly that they needed experienced help, and they began allowing certain America-Liberians to assist them in governing. One man of experience who was hired was Charles Taylor, an America-Liberian and a Gola tribesman from Nimba County. The hiring of Taylor would eventually lead to Doe's downfall.

Foreign investors stopped doing business in Liberia, and many wealthy Liberians moved their money overseas. This caused a shortage of cash. At the time the standard currency used in Liberia was the US dollar, but when the shortage of cash occurred, Doe created his own currency, which quickly depreciated on the black market.

Ronald Reagan was president of the United States during this time, and he needed an ally to try to control the spread of Soviet influence in Africa, and Liberia needed financial aid. Doe exploited this situation by closing the embassies of Libya and other socialist countries in Liberia to keep the US happy. Liberia became an important Cold War ally of the US and received millions of dollars in aid. Even after it was evident that Doe ran a police state, the US continued to subsidize one third of the Liberian government's spending from 1980 to 1985, because Doe operated as a Cold War surrogate.

Cracks in the PRC quickly began to emerge. In August 1981, Doe executed five of the original seventeen members of the PRC for allegedly plotting to assassinate him. Included in the five was Thomas Weh Syen, who was co-chair of the PRC with Doe. From 1981 through 1985, there were at least seven coup attempts against Doe. He began to only trust people from his own Krahn tribe, and he placed mostly Krahn people in government and military positions around him.

5 ~ STRUGGLES

In 1981, when I was seventeen years old, I was promoted to the fifth grade. I was struggling. Sending myself to school and taking care of myself took all my energy. I was still shining shoes from seven in the morning until noon, and then I would go get ready for school, which started at one. After school, I would take off my uniform and put on my street clothes again. I had to take care of my uniform. One set had to last for a whole school year, from March to December at that time.

From 1978 to 1981, I had done most everything for myself. However, also during this time, I found myself on the wrong path in life. I hung out with the wrong sort of people and fell into doing drugs and drinking alcohol. My bad relationships also led me to gambling. People who gambled were considered tough guys, and this was the reputation I wanted for myself. I spent a lot of time gambling.

In that year, my cousin, Wilfred Faulkner, invited me off the streets to stay with him again. When Wilfred's parents asked him where I was going to sleep, he told them I would sleep in his room. However, this arrangement worked for only a little while. He then asked his parents to allow me to fix up a small room in the house where I could sleep. The room was very small; it was essentially an open space in the back hallway of the house. I got some bricks and cement and made a little sleeping space. There was no door, so I hung a cloth over the entrance. This room was a blessing; I did not have to sleep in abandoned cars or houses that were vacant and in disrepair or in the gambling hall.

Sometimes, I shared my room with some of my street friends, and my little room became a safe haven for friends who needed a place to spend the night. However, Wilfred became angry with me once again, and I was again kicked out of the house. I went back to living on the street: working in the morning, going to school in the afternoon, finding food and a place to do my homework and somewhere to sleep at night.

Then, again, Wilfred came to me and said he was sorry and asked me to move back in with him. What could I do but agree? I again moved into the Faulkner's house. By this time, I was already hooked on weed and alcohol, and I introduced my cousin to smoking and drinking.

For his part, Wilfred really helped me out this time. He provided me with food and other things. Uncle Faulkner and my aunty told me they would feed me and give me a place to live, but I would be responsible for my schooling costs. The two biggest things I received from my uncle's household were a place to sleep and food to eat. I told my uncle and aunty that I was grateful to them, and I was very grateful to my cousin. Although we did have some bad times, at least Wilfred provided me opportunity for shelter and food.

Around this most recent time of moving back in with Wilfred, I met a new friend named David Scott who lived in the Buzzie Quarter also. David and I were in the same class at school, and David was also living with his uncle, so we had much in common. We became very close. David and I looked so much alike and were so close that people called us brothers. David later moved out of his uncle's house and went to live with another uncle in another part of Monrovia, but we stayed friends.

After David moved away, I became friends with another boy named William Pewee who was also in my class at school. We were also the same age. Pewee was a quiet guy. I did all the talking for him. He spent almost all of his time with me after school. While David was a tough guy, though not as strong as I was, Pewee was very shy.

I became close with Pewee because of his shyness and gentleness. He had no friends in our class; he was so shy that he could not take part in class discussions. I thought he was struggling, like me, so I decided to befriend him. One day, I asked him to hang out with me after school. He showed up, but I could not get him to say anything. After a couple of hours, he left for home. The next day we hung out again, and this time I went to see where he lived. I wanted to see his living conditions.

I always wanted to be a help to people I felt where neglected or struggling like I was, but this was not Pewee's case. Pewee lived with his biological parents. His father was in the military, while his mother was a housewife. He had one older sister and two younger brothers. When I went to Pewee's house, I realized he was living a much better life than me. He was with his own parents and siblings and was well taken care of. He did not have to worry about school fees, food, clothing, or other necessities as a child.

That day when we arrived at his house, he went in and brought out some food, and we ate. His mother provided extra food because I was there. His mother was such a nice lady. His father was not home; he was at work, so I did not get to meet him, but I met his older sister and younger brothers.

I had a struggle that afternoon when leaving Peewee's. I struggled with why Peewee was so shy and quiet when he was not struggling like I was. For me, I thought being with your parents and loved ones meant happiness. So why was my friend acting like someone who was neglected? I developed an interest in finding out what was going on with Peewee's attitude. In my quest to discover the reason to his quietness, I realized his siblings were much different than he was; they seemed happier and full of life. They would play around and joke with each other, while Pewee just sat and looked on.

I told myself I shouldn't be friends with Peewee, because he had almost everything but was unhappy. For me, happiness meant being with your loved ones. I wanted to be around people who struggled like I did. But while I struggled being around him, Peewee drew closer to me.

One day while we were in school, I decided I did not want to be friends with Pewee any longer, so I would not go to his house after school. After school, however, he followed me to my house, because it was our usual routine. While Pewee was in my little room waiting for us to go to his house and eat, I sneaked out to the gas station and started shining shoes. After some hours, I came back and found Pewee in my room still waiting for me. He asked me to go with him to his house. I refused, so he decided he would not go either. That night we slept at my place.

Wilfred and David joined us that night. We hung out for most of the night, but Wilfred did not sleep in my room, because he had a more comfortable bed in his room. After that night, Pewee did not sleep at his parents' house but in my little room. We only went to his parents' house to eat and came back to my place to sleep. We stayed together from fifth grade until we both completed elementary and junior high school. I taught Pewee everything I knew. I even taught him my bad habit of smoking weed. Pewee taught me how to be humble.

Unlike Pewee and I, David and I had many similarities. We were both living with an uncle, and even though his uncle took care of more of his needs, he still had to struggle with certain necessities. It was easier to identify with David because of these struggles than with Pewee, who I felt had everything.

I became a leader for David and Pewee. For Pewee, I was the older brother he never had. He loved and respected me. David was the troublemaker in our group; he would cause trouble most times we went out. Once, I had to fight for David when he caused a fight he couldn't handle. He was not as strong as I was, but he was always picking a fight. Even on the soccer field, David would often start an unnecessary argument that would lead to a fight. Pewee never participated in the fighting; he always walked away from arguments and trouble.

After some time in my uncle's house, my Aunty Faulkner began to be very good to me. She trusted me so much that I kept things for her, such as her money and her bank book. She also let me do all of her communications, including writing letters for her to her son who lived in the United States.

We called my uncle Pa and my aunty Ma. These are popular names for a husband and wife in Liberia and many other African countries. Sometimes children call their fathers Pappy, while mothers are sometimes called Old Ma. We also call an older man Uncle and an older woman Aunty. They might not be our true uncle or aunty, but for the sake of respect, these titles are used.

Ma—Aunty Faulkner—passed away during the war. May her soul, and the souls of all my friends and family members who lost their lives during the war, rest in peace.

My uncle sometimes went out to the villages, and those times we became very free. My aunty was not too harsh with us. Many times, we gambled in the room I had built at the back of the house. We slept in the room much of the time too, because it was safer than sleeping on the streets, especially on the weekends. But we often had to wait for the other gamblers to finish to collect our share of the winnings and go to sleep, and sometimes this was very late into the night.

However, every time we came home late, Ma would warn us. There were other people renting rooms in my uncle's house, and these people got mad when we came home late and knocked at the front door while they were asleep. They didn't want to leave the door unlocked for us for security reasons, and Ma said she didn't want to keep coming to open the door for us. One day she told me that me and all my friends and my cousin needed to fix up the small outside kitchen, separate from the main house, and use it as our room.

The idea of fixing up the little outside kitchen as a room seemed like a great idea to me; I was up for it. The kitchen had no door and no concrete floor, but I didn't care. I used to sleep in cars and open places, so having any room was a great blessing, even though the kitchen's roof leaked during the rainy season. The roof leaked because the zinc was old. Zinc was what we called the metal sheets we often used for the roof of a house. They actually were made out of tin.

The day after Ma told me about fixing up the kitchen, I decided to collect sand from the beach to cover the floor of the room. I also collected cardboard and used it to soak up the puddles of water, and I used cardboard for beds and placed it over the leaky zinc roof as well. I was able to hang a small door too, so all the stuff we kept in the room would not be stolen. My cousin still had his little room in the house, so we kept all our most important stuff in his room and slept in the kitchen whenever we came home late. I worked very hard on fixing up my little kitchen room. By the time I was done, many of my friends joined me in my room. Because of that little room, I became very popular and powerful. Many boys slept with us there during the dry season from November to April.

The password to get into my room was "spoon," because we used a spoon as a key to open the door. Because of this, my room became known as Mr. Spoon Shop, and this name became very popular in the community. We turned the room into a place for gambling. Many gamblers, big and small, came to gamble, and of course, I would collect money from everyone who gambled in my room. The money I collected was used to improve my room, if I did not lose it on the gambling board.

We played a card game called *palapy*. It is a card game that requires two to six persons to play. Each person is dealt three cards. Players need to find a pair by drawing a card (called plucking in Liberia) from the deck or using the top card on the discard pile to match with cards in their hands. Players do not allow anyone to see what cards they have until someone wins. A player wins a hand by matching all of the cards in his hand and laying them down. This game is well known in Liberia, and many people, young and old, play it.

In *palapy*, players decide how much they want to bet on each hand. As for us, we played for five or ten cents per hand. The money is kept by a banker, who does not play that hand. The banker pays whoever wins the hand and is paid for acting as banker whenever one player wins two times in a row, for us, usually five cents. Players can also have side bets. We would bet five cents or more on who might get the first match in a hand. A side bet can be continued by betting on who might get the second match, and so on.

Because Mr. Spoon Shop was mine, I was often the banker. When I was not the banker, each player had to pay me before he was allowed to enter. This is how I made money from hosting the gambling, and sometimes I also played.

During the rainy season (from May to October), it was hard to sleep in my room in the small kitchen. The room would fill with water every time it rained. In order to sleep, I took concrete blocks and laid them on top of each other then put planks and sticks over the blocks then placed cartons over the planks and sticks so I had a high bed I could climb onto. It is very hard to explain this arrangement. Many people will not understand or be able to picture the sort of bed I am trying to describe, but those who lived in Monrovia at that time will know what I am talking about.

In 1983, when I was nineteen, I graduated from the sixth grade from Lorma Quarter Elementary. Lorma Quarter Elementary was originally named Kezzel Kollie Total Involvement Elementary, after Kezzel Kollie, the powerful, wealthy, and uneducated Lorma governor who lived in the Buzzie Quarter with his many children and multiple wives and built the school, which was the first in the community. For political reasons, Kollie later dedicated the school to William R. Tolbert, the president of Liberia at the time, and later the name was changed again to Lorma Quarter Elementary School.

After graduating from elementary school, I went to G. W. Gibson Junior High School, located near Capital Bypass in Monrovia. I had to walk to school every day, but the distance from where I lived in the Buzzie Quarter to my new school was not too far for me. This was another government school and not too expensive, but I still shined shoes or washed cars every day to make money for my schooling and for food. William Pewee went to G. W. Gibson with me. We were both in seventh grade. Wilfred also went to the school, but he was in ninth grade. I was eighteen months older than Wilfred, but he was ahead of me in school, because he started school before I did.

During my junior high years, things were still very difficult for me. I didn't want to shine shoes or wash cars anymore, because my friends from school would laugh at me if they knew I was doing that sort of work, so I didn't tell them; I didn't want girls to know I was a shoe-shine boy or a car washer either. People who did this sort of work were considered street people. Because of my friends laughing at me, I decided not to do this sort of work anymore.

My decision to not do street work anymore made things even harder on me. I could not afford to buy food or other things for myself. So I got more involved in gambling. Also, when I was sure all my friends had gone home, I would sometimes still go out and wash cars at night. I became a midnight taxicab washer. I did this for some time, but the outcome was that I slept during class. My friends again started laughing at me. They began teasing me and calling me names like Midnight Mover and Pappy. In the end, however, I still had friends because I was smart and received good grades and I completed homework assignments for most of my friends. Girls still liked me too.

Around this time, there was a lawyer who rented a room in my Uncle Faulkner's house. This lawyer had two boys. One day he asked me if I wanted to work for him, and I agreed to work for him for fifteen dollars per month. My job was to take his two boys to school every day and bring them back home. I was also responsible to buy food for them. This was good for me because I ate some of the boys' food also. I did this work until the lawyer's wife came home to her husband and, after a few months, decided to hire her brother to do my job. The brother who she hired to take my place came to be my friend. Unfortunately, I do not remember his name. He used to share his food with me, but not his money.

After that, I began to wash people's clothes for a living. I also opened study classes for children in my community. I did not get paid for teaching—sometimes a little money—but some of the parents did give me food. But I could not keep up with teaching because I could not keep regular hours. Often, I went to play soccer in the afternoon, and by the time I was done playing, it was already too late for class. The children I taught were smaller, so their parents could not allow them to stay out late. Eventually, another boy took over my study class, because he was available during the day, but he collected money from parents for each child.

I also became friends with an older businessman who sold beef. His name was Genesis Gayflor. He would buy a cow, kill it, then sell the meat. I got to know Genesis through a lady who also rented a room from my uncle. This lady would send me to the market place to buy meat and other things for her. When Genesis came to visit the lady, he would send me to buy beer for him. The lady did not drink any alcohol, so I would buy beer for Genesis and a soft drink for the lady. I became their errand runner. Often times Genesis would tell me to keep his change and his leftover food. Then one day, Genesis told me that he was going to open a small provision shop and he wanted me to work there. I eagerly accepted the offer.

Genesis opened his shop in 1986, and I began working there. I could not run the shop on my own because I had to go to school, so one of my older cousins, James Gono, was asked to work in the shop too. I went to school in the morning and worked in the evening. James worked at the shop during the day and went to night school. James was struggling like I was, but his older brother and sister were able to help him out a little. His older brother was a police officer, so he had some income, and his older sister was married, and they both helped him with some occasional cash.

Genesis paid us in the beginning. My cousin got twenty dollars and I got fifteen dollars every month. Eventually, he stopped paying us, however, so my cousin decided to leave. I was left alone to do all the work. I would close the shop while I was in school, and after school, around one in the afternoon, I would open the shop again for business. I was hoping Genesis would see my dedication to him and start to pay me again. But he did not.

Genesis did not pay me for my work in the shop for almost an entire year—the reason I continued to worked for him was I at least had food to eat every day. Genesis would come and get his money from the day's sales and spend the money on girlfriends. He would call to order beer from the shop but would not pay for it, so his business started going down.

One day, I told Genesis I could not continue working for him because he was not paying me and was spending all the money I made for him on women. I told him he needed to come to the shop so we could check the inventory and prepare for me to turn it over to him. He came along with a friend, and we looked over the inventory. After checking everything, he told me he was sorry for not paying me, but he wanted me to stay on and work for him at another one of his businesses. The man he brought with him also asked me to stay and work for his friend. I agreed to continue to work for Genesis, but I told him he needed to promise to pay me.

My new job for Genesis was working at his night club and bar called the Base. This job was something I really enjoyed because it was fun. Also, I wanted to get to know people, and I wanted people to get to know me. I felt the job would make people respect me and see me as someone they could trust.

Work at the Base started out well, and I loved to play music as the DJ there. The location was very good for business, but because Genesis did not pay his rent, the owner of the building asked us to leave. I was out of a job again, so I went back to my usual life of struggling to survive.

Because I met many people during the time I worked at the Base, I started hanging out with guys and girls my age in night clubs. Drinking and womanizing became my new occupation. Almost every night we went to the night club. Life once again turned upside down for me. I began smoking, drinking, and gambling again. It was a bad life. I carried on with this kind of life for some time. I do thank God that at least I never took part in stealing or causing serious trouble.

One thing that helped me out during this time was I was very strong. It was not easy for another boy or man to take me down in a fight. I would fight anyone, and I won most of these fights. Girls felt safe hanging out with me, because I could defend them from the street fighting, so they took me out and provided drinks for me. I did not look for fights, but if anyone took advantage of a girl or any older woman or man, I would fight that person, no matter whether I knew the person they were taking advantage of or not.

However, these acts of defending people eventually took me to jail.

There was a lady named Gertrude who lived in my Uncle Faulkner's house with her husband, James, who was a friend of mine, and James's nephew, Amah. James was in the Liberian Coast Guard, and Gertrude ran a little market in front of my uncle's house selling peanuts, candy, table salt, red palm oil, and other small items. Gertrude was a very quiet woman, and she sometimes would help some of us out with food.

One particular afternoon, I was sitting in front of the house where Gertrude was running her little market, and Amah was sitting with some of us there too. After a while, a lady approached Gertrude. This lady was very drunk, and she started giving Gertrude trouble. Gertrude kept telling this lady to leave her alone, but the drunken lady just kept on abusing her. She wanted to destroy Gertrude's little market, so I ran to help protect Gertrude and her business. Amah was sitting there watching but would not get up to help protect his uncle's wife. Eventually, I managed to move this drunken lady away, and then I walked her all the way to her home.

When I came back to my uncle's house, Gertrude was talking heatedly to Amah about the way he had behaved to her. She told Amah she would tell James about his attitude when James came home from work. She said if I had not been there to help her, she would have lost all her goods. She was so angry with Amah, she started crying. I told her to forget about it and wait for her husband to come home from work. Then I left to play soccer.

While I was playing soccer, I saw a boy named Amara coming toward the field. Amara rented a room from my uncle too, and we sometimes used his room to gamble and smoke weed and cigarettes. His room was paid for by his uncle, but his uncle did not live there with him. Amara's uncle was a kind man, and Amara was very blessed that his uncle took good care of him and did almost everything for him.

That day, Amara came at me, accosting and insulting me. I asked him why he was angry with me, and he told me it was because of what I had done in his room. He said Amah had told him I used his room to have an affair with a drunken woman. I told him if I was able to prove the story was untrue, I was going to fight him. Amara agreed.

We all left the soccer field and headed toward my uncle's house. When we got there, we met Gertrude and Amah. I asked Amara to tell us who told him I had taken a drunken woman into his room. He told everybody standing there that it had been Amah. I asked Amah if this was true, and he said yes, he had told Amara the story. I asked Amah what I should do to him if it was proven he was lying.

One of the older men who lived in my uncle's house headed up the investigation, and it was proven that Amah was lying. So I told Amara to get ready to fight. I was very serious about fighting. It was my way of life. Amara apologized to me and asked me to forget it. I agreed to forgive Amara but decided to fight Amah. During the fight, I wounded Amah badly. He was bleeding from his ear, and I left him lying in front of the house.

Because Amah's uncle, James, was in the Coast Guard, after he learned about the fight, he went to the police. It was Christmas vacation, so the next morning, I left the house early to go on the hustle, to look for a way to make money. When I came home that evening, I went straight to my room. My friend and I were sitting in my room when we heard a knock on the door. My friend said it might be the police, but I told him, "Oh, stop." But sure enough, he was right. When I opened the door, I saw that James had brought four policemen to have me arrested. They told me I was needed at the police station for an investigation over how Amah became wounded. I was taken and put behind bars.

Gertrude asked her husband to have me released, but he refused. I was kept in jail for eight days, and no one came to release me. My uncle did not help me because, he said, I had acted stupidly. Gertrude kept after James to have me released because I had helped save her business. After eight days, he agreed but under one condition, which was I pay all of Amah's medical bills. Amah's bills totaled about fifty dollars, and this was a lot of money for me to come up with. However, Uncle Faulkner came to the police station and signed the agreement, and I was released on the eighth day at about three in the afternoon.

During this time, from 1983 to 1986, President Samuel Doe began to crack down on the members of those tribal people he thought were against him.

Thomas Quiwonkpa was a Gio from Nimba County in northern Liberia. He was one of the leaders of the 1980 coup against President Tolbert and was a member of the PRC. After the coup, he was made the commanding general of the six-thousand-member Armed Forces of Liberia (AFL). He wanted to return Liberia to a democracy, but Doe wanted to continue ruling the country himself. Doe demoted Quiwonkpa, resulting in a major conflict between the two leaders, and in 1983, Quiwonkpa fled the country, fearing for his life. Many other Gio left the country as well during this time. Also during this time, Charles Taylor fled to the United States, because Doe had accused him of embezzling $900,000 from the Liberian government and ordered his arrest.

Prince Johnson, Quiwonkpa's aide-de-camp, also fled Liberia and joined Quiwonkpa in the Ivory Coast. Johnson would later become a warlord during the Liberian Civil War and fight against Doe. Quiwonkpa and his military supporters began staging raids from the Ivory Coast into Nimba County, where they attacked government offices. The Ivory Coast did nothing to prevent these raids, in large part because the president of the Ivory Coast, Felix Houphouet-Boigny, had pleaded for mercy from Doe for his son-in-law, Benedick Tolbert, who was the son of President Tolbert and had been a member of his cabinet. But Doe had shown no mercy and executed Benedick during the coup.

Doe feared the Gio people would attempt a rebellion against him led by Quiwonkpa. In an attempt to destroy Quiwonkpa's base of support in 1984, the Liberian Army carried out what was called the Nimba Raid in Nimba County, where many Gio still lived. Thousands of innocent people were killed, villages were burned, and many fled into exile. Many people from Nimba County fled to the Ivory Coast to escape the brutal reign of terror against them.

Also in 1984, many students and some of the staff of the University of Liberia began to publicly oppose Doe's leadership. This made Doe furious. Doe had some of the university staff and student leaders arrested. When this happened, the students boycotted classes, and Doe sent in the army. The army sealed off the Monrovia University of Liberia campus and began a five-day rampage of rape, torture, and murder against the students and staff.

Doe's government continued to become increasingly corrupt and repressive. Doe continued to ban political opposition; he shut down newspapers and jailed reporters. He eliminated anyone who opposed him. In an attempt to appease international aid organizations that provided funding to Liberia, Doe did agree to allow national elections, and a new Liberian Constitution was drafted and approved by a legislature of mostly Doe supporters.

But in an almost comical twist, this new constitution was patterned after the US Constitution, which states that the president must be thirty-five years old. Doe was only thirty-four at the time, so he issued a decree changing his age to thirty-six.

Doe staged a presidential election in October 1985. A total of nine political parties formed, but the government only allowed three candidates to run for office. Doe threatened anyone who opposed him with arrest and detained several of his presidential rivals on fabricated charges. All fifty-six thousand government employees were required to support Doe's political party or face being fired. Independent observers and foreign correspondents called the election results fraudulent because teams of observers were barred from many polling places. Soldiers loyal to Doe confiscated many ballot boxes and had the ballots counted by Krahn tribesmen, and Liberian television showed scenes of delayed returns of ballot boxes and at least one batch of ballots discovered in a smoldering heap north of the capital. However, in the end, Doe declared himself the winner of the election with 51 percent of the vote.

Soon after the election results were reported, on November 12, 1985, a group of five to six hundred rebels led by Thomas Quiwonkpa, mostly from the Gio and Mano tribes from Nimba County, attempted to seize power from Doe. Quiwonkpa infiltrated Monrovia and seized the military barracks, the Barclay Training Center, and the state-run radio station, where he broadcasted that he was now in control of the country. People ran into the streets and began to celebrate their deliverance from Doe. Crowds tore down billboards of Doe and danced and sang songs of praise for their deliverers.

However, Doe had not been routed or captured, and he soon rallied nearby troops loyal to him and retook the radio station and the barracks. The attempted coup barely lasted one day. The carnage that followed was indescribable—troops loyal to Doe sought out every Monrovian who had celebrated Quiwonkpa's short-lived rebellion and slaughtered them. Television and reporters' cameras had captured the celebrating, and Doe used these images to identify everyone who was involved in the celebrating and kill them.

Quiwonkpa was caught, castrated, and beaten to death. His dismembered body was displayed publicly. Some of the Krahn soldiers ate parts of his body, believing that by doing this, some of the greatness of Quiwonkpa would pass to them. I remember seeing one of Doe's soldiers carrying one of Quiwonkpa's hands and other body parts around Monrovia. However, Doe did not stop there. He sent his troops into Nimba County, where Quiwonkpa was from, and massacred thousands more civilians from the Gio and Mano tribes.

Now that Quiwonkpa was dead, the streets of Monrovia were very quiet. There was no one to challenge Doe. Many people, especially those not belonging to Doe's government or his Krahn tribe, cried out for justice, but no one heard them. If you were Doe's friend, you were safe, but if you spoke against Doe, everyone knew you would likely be killed. Doe was now a dictator.

Doe was sworn in as President on January 6, 1986.

From 1986 to 1990, the government of Liberia unleashed a reign of terror on the people. Many people were arrested, many people disappeared, and many people were killed because they opposed Doe. Mismanagement, corruption, and abuse of human rights became rampant at an unprecedented level, and many international businesses left Liberia. Many Liberian professionals also fled the country.

During this time, the church tried to bring peace between Doe and political opposition leaders, but this did not work. Doe was now very powerful and willing to protect himself and his government at any cost, and he became enraged when anyone opposed him. The government openly criticized the church, suspended subsidies to church related health and educational institutions, and targeted pastors who preached against the evil practices of his administration and threatened them with public floggings.

During this time, I was a young man focused on earning a living and pursuing an education. I needed to earn enough money every day to eat and pay for my schooling. These were my priorities.

After we graduated from junior high school, Pewee left my Uncle Faulkner's home and went to live with his uncle who had the finances to put him through private school. I could not afford private school, so I enrolled at a government school. After Pewee, left we were not as close, but David and I stayed close, even though we went to different schools after we were promoted to tenth grade. Then when the both of us were promoted to the eleventh grade, we decided to go to the same school again, Well's Hairstone High School.

At the end of eleventh grade, in 1988, neither David nor I could afford to pay our school fees, so we dropped out. I spent that whole year earning money for the following school year so I could complete my high school education. I did not earn enough money in 1988 to support my schooling the following year, but I told myself I must complete high school in 1989 some way.

I decided to talk to Mr. Boimah, the principal at Well's Hairstone, about my situation. Mr. Boimah had been very good to me. At the end of eleventh grade, he had allowed me to write my final exams even though I could not pay the balance of my school fees.

I went to Mr. Boimah's office, and he was happy to see me. He asked where I had been the whole year and why I had not been at school. I explained my situation, and he was angry I had not considered telling him about what was going on sooner. He told me he could have helped.

"Well, that is gone," he said. "What do you want me to do for you now?" I told him that I wanted him to give me my report card and to help me enroll in the night section, because I couldn't afford the morning section fees. Mr. Boimah freed my report card and recommended me to the night school principal for enrollment. I enrolled that year and completed high school in December 1989, when the Liberian Civil War started.

I have not seen Mr. Boimah since the war. I hope he's alive.

Pewee graduated from high school a year earlier than I did, because I had dropped out for a year. Pewee is still a friend, but we are not as close as we used to be. David refused to attend night school, but he managed to graduate in December 1989 also. Unfortunately, David was killed in the war. He ended up fighting for one of the rebel factions, the Liberia Peace Council, and died on the battlefield, according to some accounts I received. May the soul of my dear friend and brother David rest in peace. Wilfred has returned to Liberia from Guinea, where he took refuge during the war. He now lives at his parents' house in the Buzzie Quarter. However, both my Uncle and Aunty Faulkner died during the war, though from natural causes. Wilfred and I are still in contact.

Once Charles Taylor returned to Africa and the war began, I was relatively safe, because I am from the Kpelle tribe. We were not targeted during the war. The Kpelle tribe is very peaceful and respectful. This is well known in Liberia. A rebel even confessed this to me when I was arrested for the first time during the war in 1990. The leader of the rebels told his men to allow me and my friends to go because we were Kpelle. He said, "Leave those Kpelle people. We came for Doe and his Krahn people." Even though we were not targeted, all tribes suffered greatly during the war.

At the beginning of the war, Charles Taylor specifically targeted president Doe's tribe, the Krahn, and his entire government. Doe's forces had committed many atrocities against Taylor's Gola tribe. Other tribes, such as the Lorma, Bassa, Grebo, and a few others, enjoyed relative freedom of movement throughout the country. But there were certain tribes who couldn't go certain places. Taylor claimed he was only coming for the president, his tribal men, and those in his government, but this proved to be untrue. As the war went on, things got out of hand, and the rebels began expressing personal grudges against people they felt had mistreated them. Even teachers who had punished or humiliated students before the war were either humiliated or killed by those students who had turned soldiers.

I believe the entire Liberian Civil War was mostly a lot of greedy and ignorant men wrongly expressing themselves. No government or military leader in fourteen years did anything for the good of the people of Liberia. The leaders involved in the war were only out to benefit themselves by robbing the treasury and the people of every dollar to build themselves mansions, purchase fancy cars, and travel the world.

6 ~ MY LIFE IS CHANGED

While I was in jail for wounding Amah, I had made up my mind to never fight again. After I was released, I went and took a bath in the ocean and asked God to wash my sin away. I was done with my life outside of Christ. I cut off all my hair as a sign to my friends that I was a changed person and I was never going to fight again, no matter what. I decided I was going to start attending church. But I did not have clothes to go to church in. Sunday is a very special day for Christians in Liberia. For us, going to church means putting on a nice set of clothes, but I had no money to purchase nice clothes. I really wanted to change my ways and do the right thing, and I felt that going to church was the best option for me if I wanted to be a good man.

I had made a good decision, but I had a problem. That problem was how to survive. How could I attend church when I had to go to the night clubs to gamble to make money? I knew very well what it meant to be a practicing Christian. It meant I had to leave behind all my gambling, smoking, drinking, and sex. However, with these conflicts in mind, I followed through on my decision to start attending church.

I started by attending a Bible study—which I did not have to dress up for—that met in the Buzzie Quarter every Wednesday evening. I became a regular, and the leader of the Bible study, William Karbo, became my good friend. Karbo knew my story, and he was told many times by some of the boys and girls who attended the Bible study that I was doing bad things, but he continued to mentor me in the ways of the Lord. Many of the boys and girls in the Bible study teased me constantly and joked about me. Every meeting they told me I was not a good Christian because I was still involved in worldly things. Because of this, I decided to give up on going to Bible study and to church. Karbo tried to continue a presence in my life, but every time I saw him looking for me, I ran away.

Gambling again became my way to survive, and my small four-by- four-foot room in the kitchen behind the Faulkner's house again became the best gambling spot for me and my friends. There was always a lot of smoking and drinking around the gambling board, and there was fighting. Cheating always caused fights. Because of the fights, I came up with two rules: cheating was not allowed, and no one was allowed to fight in my room. I was able to enforce these rules because I was strong and had a reputation as a fighter. If anyone was caught cheating or fighting in my room, they were not allowed back.

It took some time after I became a Christian to leave gambling, and it was Christ who set me free. One day as we were gambling in my room, an evangelist, Pastor Dennis Gaye, came and asked us if he could pray for us. We agreed, so Pastor Gaye asked us to bow our heads, and he prayed for us. When he was through, he invited us to attend his Bible study, which was usually held in the Buzzie Quarter. Some of us agreed to attend, but when the day of the Bible study came, we chose to gamble instead.

After we skipped the Bible study, Pastor Gaye came back to see us and pleaded with us to attend the next meeting. He continued to invite us to Bible study and church almost every week for roughly a year. One day, David and I had finally decided to attend the Bible study, but then Pastor Gaye again came to my room behind Uncle Faulkner's house and told us that week, instead of Bible study, they were having a revival at the community school building, and he wanted us to go. We were gambling when Pastor Gaye showed up and asked us to go with him, but David and I decided to follow him to the revival meeting. We went and sat together.

At the revival, the preacher was a man from Freetown, Sierra Leone, and it was his first time in Liberia, but David and I did not know this. Every time the preacher spoke about drugs, gambling, and other sins, we felt he was speaking directly against us, so we became angry. I said to David it sounded like this man knew us well. It appeared he knew all our doings, our gambling, smoking, and bad ways of living. Both of us were so angry that we wanted to walk right out of the meeting. But because there were so many people and the preacher was still talking, we were too ashamed to walk out. We decided to wait until the preacher was done with his message and then leave and never come back to that church again.

We waited for the preacher to finish speaking. But while we were trying to make our escape, Pastor Gaye, who had invited us, came over and asked us about the sermon. I told him that we were feeling very angry. He asked us why, and we told him the preacher had spoken against us. Then Pastor Gaye asked us how we knew the preacher was speaking against us specifically. We said all the bad things he spoke about were our own sins. Every time the preacher spoke about sin, his finger rested on us. We felt like the preacher knew us well. How could he know all about our gambling, smoking, and sexual lives?

Pastor Gaye told us it had not been the preacher speaking about us, but it had been the Holy Spirit speaking to us. He asked us to sit down so he could explain more about the Holy Spirit. It was during this discussion we were told the preacher was not from Liberia but from Freetown and this was his very first time visiting Liberia. Pastor Gaye spoke to us for some time, explaining the work and power of the Holy Spirit. Then he asked us if we wanted to accept Jesus Christ as our Lord and Savior. Then and there, David and I both decided to give our lives to Christ. Pastor Gaye said with us the Sinner's Prayer. The Sinner's Prayer is a confession of sins and a request for Christ to come into your heart as your Lord and Savior. There is not an official Sinner's Prayer, and there are many examples. You can simply pray to God in your own words if you choose. David and I, following Pastor Gaye, prayed something like this:

Dear God,

I come to You in the name of Jesus. I acknowledge to You that I am a sinner, and I am sorry for my sins and the life I have lived; I ask for Your forgiveness. I believe Jesus is God's only Son who shed His blood on the cross at Calvary and died for my sins, and I am now willing to turn from my sin.

The Bible states in Romans 10:9, if we believe in our hearts that God raised Jesus from the dead and confess Jesus as our Lord and Savior, we shall be saved.

With all my heart, I believe God raised Jesus from the dead. And I confess Jesus as my Lord and Savior. This very moment I accept Jesus Christ as my own personal Savior and, according to His Word, as of this moment I am saved.

Thank You, Jesus, for Your unlimited grace, which has saved me from my sins.

Amen.

Once we had prayed, Pastor Gaye told us we were now brand-new Christians and, because we were now Christians, we needed to start attending Bible studies and church services regularly. Every week, Pastor Gaye would find us and encourage us in the Word of God. Pastor Gaye became so very close to me, and I felt I had someone who wanted me to know real life, and real life is in Christ.

Remember, we were well known by people in the Buzzie Quarter, especially by the youth, because we were still young ourselves. We were well known because of our previous lives of fighting, gambling, and womanizing. When the community learned David and I were now attending church regularly, many people felt we would never keep it up. Every time people saw us going to Bible study or church, they would stop us and ask us if we were really serious about all of it. Yes, indeed, we were very serious about our new lives. Giving my life to Christ truly helped shape who I am today. It was not easy, but I was determined to change. And Pastor Gaye continued to be a very big part of this change.

I thank the Lord for the blessing of Pastor Dennis Gaye. Because of his influence and help, I grew in my faith. He took me on many evangelical missions around the Buzzie Quarter and to neighboring communities around Monrovia. Slowly but surely, I started to get rid of the bad habits that had enslaved me, and my life began to change for the better as, more and more, I began to lead a life rooted in the Word of God.

Pastor Gaye was killed during the Liberian Civil War, but I will always remember him as my mentor and spiritual father. I believe God brought him into my life to help shape me. May his soul rest in peace.

During the late 1980s, the world and Liberia were also going through radical changes. With the end of the Cold War in sight, Doe's usefulness to American interests also came to an end. The US House of Representatives and the US Senate passed nonbinding resolutions tying aid to Liberia to progress in human rights and true democracy. In 1986, US aid to Liberia was $53.6 million, but by 1989, it had dropped to $19.5 million. International aid organizations were also withdrawing their support from Liberia, putting tremendous stress on the economy. Meanwhile, Liberians who had fled to other African nations from the Doe regime were starting to unite under the common goal of removing him from power.

In 1983, Charles Taylor had fled for his life to the United States, where he was arrested and jailed in 1984 for extradition to Liberia for allegedly embezzling money from the Liberian government while in the employment of the Doe regime. He spent fifteen months in jail while his attorney, former US Attorney General Ramsey Clark, fought for his release.

Taylor escaped from his maximum-security prison in 1985— under suspicious circumstances. Supposedly, Taylor convinced a guard to bend the rules to allow him to pass from one wing of the jail to another, where he used a hacksaw to cut through the bars of a window and lowered himself to the ground using bedsheets. It is known Taylor was recruited by the CIA in the early 1980s, and he claims it was the CIA who helped him escape. Taylor made his way to Ghana, West Africa, via Mexico and then spent time traveling throughout West Africa, cultivating the relationships he needed to achieve his plan to remove Doe from the presidency.

Taylor was introduced to Libyan leader Muammar Qaddafi in late 1987, who allowed Taylor to train troops in Libya. Qaddafi held a grudge against Doe because Doe had previously closed the Libyan Embassy in Liberia to appease the US—this resulted in Qaddafi losing face in the Arab world. And Qaddafi was extremely anti-American for a number of reasons: Qaddafi had approved the bombing of a Berlin nightclub in 1986, and the US responded by bombing his Libyan residence, which resulted in the death of one of his daughters. And in 1987, the Libyan Army was defeated in their invasion of Chad by the Chadian Army, which was supported by US and French forces.

Qaddafi saw his support of Taylor as an opportunity to attack the United States through Liberia, where the CIA still operated a large base from which they had coordinated the Chadian Army attacks against Qaddafi's forces. Once Taylor secured Qaddafi's support, he was able to place himself in a position of power between the international backers of a revolt against Doe and the Liberian exiles who would form the core of his army.

Taylor was related through marriage to Thomas Quiwonkpa, and many of Quiwonkpa's former followers were drawn to Taylor. Prince Johnson, Quiwonkpa's former aide de camp, brought many trained soldiers with him when he fled to the Ivory Coast, and he joined his forces with Taylor's. Taylor took the name of his army from that which Quiwonkpa had used for his forces: the National

Patriotic Front of Liberia (NPFL). This was to encourage Gio and Mano tribesmen to join his cause. Many Gio and Mano were eager to kill Krahn and Mandingos to avenge the savage murders of their families and kinsmen ordered by Doe.

I am so grateful the Lord saved me before the Liberian Civil War started in 1989. If he had not, I probably would have joined the fighting.

7 ~ WAR

The Liberian Civil War started on Christmas Eve 1989. The war started in Nimba County, and it took some time for the fighting to reach Monrovia. However, in Monrovia, there were still many secret killings by government soldiers of anyone suspected of being against Doe.

I don't feel good remembering those war days, and I don't like to talk about them.

When the war started, David decided to join the Armed Forces of Liberia. He later left the AFL and joined the Liberia Peace Council. David made his decision, in part, because things were so difficult during those days that only those in the military could get enough food to eat. Soldiers could loot food from citizens because they carried guns.

David wanted both of us to join the AFL, but I refused. I did not want to take part in the fighting. I felt strongly that war was not the way to end the conflict, especially because we all belonged to one country, and now that I was a Christian, I believed the Bible spoke against the unjust killing of another person, and I believed this war was unjust. Many of my friends who became soldiers asked me to join them, but I always refused.

David and I were roommates at the time, and one day David told me he was not going to help me or give me any of the food he was able to loot anymore because I did not want to join him and be a soldier. He said because I felt I was more holy than he was and more Christian, he did not want to be around me. Because I continued to refuse to become a soldier, David moved out and moved in with another friend who was a soldier. From that time on, David called me Reverend.

When David died, I was told he was killed in battle, but someone also told me it was one of David's friends who killed him for all the things David had stolen while looting. David and I gave our lives to Jesus on the same day. We attended the same church, African Christian Fellowship International (ACFI), and we were baptized also on the same day. He was my brother. May his soul rest in peace.

On December 24, 1989, Charles Taylor invaded Liberia from the Ivory Coast with an armed force of around 150 soldiers. These soldiers were mainly from Liberia and Burkina Faso and had trained in Libya. President Boigny of the Ivory Coast still wanted revenge against Doe for killing his son-in-law in the 1980 coup, so he helped Taylor by allowing his troops to fly into the Ivory Coast from Burkina Faso and invade Liberia from their common border.

Burkina Faso supported Taylor with arms and troops. President Blaise Compaoré of Burkina Faso had become the leader of Burkina Faso in a coup in 1987 supported by exiled Liberian troops, including Prince Johnson, and was married to the foster sister of President Tolbert's widow. Military supplies and manpower from Libya and Burkina Faso arrived in the Ivory Coast and were sent to Liberia from there. Taylor's personal body guards were from Burkina Faso.

Taylor moved across the Ivory Coast border into Butuo, Nimba County, where he attacked government offices and personnel. Because the attack took place over the Christmas holiday, it took many people by surprise. On January 1, 1990, the BBC broadcasted a declaration from Charles Taylor stating he had invaded Liberia without any political ambitions except to remove Doe from the presidency. He urged Liberians to take up arms against Doe.

Doe reacted slowly to the invasion. On December 29, 1989, he sent tanks and troops to Nimba County. The Liberian Army had around six thousand soldiers at this time, so Doe did not think an invasion of around 150 men required a major response. However, he misjudged the level of resentment against his regime and the loyalty of his own troops. Taylor's group, the National Patriotic Front of Liberia, attracted thousands of Gio and Mano tribesmen and many Americo-Liberians. They were eager to exact revenge against Doe, the Krahn, and the Mandingo. The Liberian Army was defeated, but not before hundreds of civilians were killed by government and NPFL soldiers.

Many of the new recruits to the NPFL were children, some as young as eight years old. They were mostly orphans, and many of their parents had been killed by government soldiers. They were made into fighting units called Small Boy Units, or SBUs, and they were exceptionally loyal to Charles Taylor. He gave them a way to avenge their parents.

In May 1990, Taylor attacked and captured Gbarnga and made it his headquarters. On May 19, he captured the port city of Buchanan, Liberia's second largest city, where hundreds of Krahn and Mandingo civilians had taken refuge—they were slaughtered by the NPFL. Taylor's forces grew quickly as dissidents of the Doe regime joined them. Most of the young people from the Gio or Mano tribes in the Buzzie Quarter left for fear they might be killed by Doe's soldiers, and many, I'm sure, joined the NPFL. The NPFL's forces swelled to an estimated ten thousand soldiers, while the Liberian Army dwindled to roughly two thousand men.

Doe's Liberian Army was now forcefully recruiting young men. Many young men in Monrovia were forced to join, while many others fled from Doe to Charles Taylor. In addition, we in Monrovia heard inviting news from the areas of Liberia that Charles Taylor now controlled. We heard Taylor was taking care of the people in these areas, distributing food and supplies to the people there. This news enticed many to flee Monrovia to these areas, but it was all lies.

Of the people who fled the fighting, many fled to other countries, such as Guinea, the Ivory Coast, Sierra Leone, Ghana, and other parts of Africa. Those who had money fled to Europe and America. Of course, those who had money were often the most educated, so this was a major intellectual drain on Liberia. Still, as of 2017, Liberia has very few doctors, dentists, and other educated and trained professionals.

The fighting eventually moved closer to Monrovia, and this resulted in an even larger exodus of people from the city. But leaving the city was not a safe thing to do. Government soldiers and the rebels established roadblocks on every road leading from Monrovia. Many people were pulled from the checkpoint lines and accused of being either a rebel or government sympathizer and were shot or bayoneted to death. Entire families were eliminated. Women were taken from the lines and gang-raped in front of their relatives. Pregnant women would have their bellies cut open as soldiers guessed the sex of the baby. Everyone had their belongings looted.

I refused to leave Monrovia. My Uncle Faulkner had already

returned to Yowee and was there when the war broke out. There was no way for him to come back to the city. Aunty Faulkner later told all of us she was leaving the house and going to her parents' village outside of Monrovia. Before she left, she asked me to take my uncle's children he had by another woman to their mother.

I agreed to take my uncle's children, Jatu and Mbangda, to their mother, who lived twenty miles outside of Monrovia in Bensonville. When we arrived, their mother asked me to spend the night and leave the next day. But something inside me kept telling me not to spend the night there, so I decided not to. The same car that took us to Bensonville had not yet left, so I jumped back into the car and headed back to Monrovia. I was blessed to be in that car that night, because it was the last car able to leave Bensonville and make it back to Monrovia. All other cars in the area had been stripped by soldiers until they were useless.

My cousin, James Gono, and I were left in charge of my Uncle Faulkner's house in the Buzzie Quarter, close to the executive mansion where President Doe was still living. I still refused to take up arms for any faction in the war, but James was now a bodyguard for President Doe, and he was always on the battlefront. So I was left in charge of the house, and his family as well. He brought food home for us when he could then returned to the front. I prayed for James every day. His wife, Martha, was always willing to share with other needy people. Everyone called her Children's Mother, because of her goodness and help to so many. James and Martha treated me very well during those hard times.

James was in Doe's Special Anti-Terrorist Unit. This unit was formed to protect Doe and was one of his most dependable fighting forces. Most of the Special Anti-Terrorist Unit's leaders were Doe's relatives and personal friends from the Krahn tribe, and were very loyal to him. Many soldiers in the Special Anti-Terrorist Unit had been trained in Israel, but James was trained in Liberia. Also, James was not Krahn, but he was a very loyal, committed, and dependable soldier for Doe. This is a common trait of the Kpelle people. When a Kpelle person gives his or her loyalty to someone, he or she will always go the extra mile.

God saved my life many times through James. People constantly tried to force me to take up arms, but I always refused. When I told them James, who was considered to be like an older brother to me, was a special forces soldier for Doe, they would let me go instantly. All of the credit of saving my life goes to the Lord God, but I must also recognize those the Lord used in the process. God works through people to help other people, but it is God from whom all blessings flow. I could have died many times during the Liberian Civil War, but God saved my life through people like my cousin, James Gono.

By July 1990, Liberia was divided into three parts. Prince Johnson, who used to fight for Charles Taylor, now led a faction called the Independent National Patriotic Front of Liberia (INPFL), which controlled Freeport and Bushrod Island. The largest part of Liberia was controlled by Charles Taylor and his NPFL. They held everything outside of Monrovia and Freeport and most of the Liberian interior. Doe controlled Monrovia, where most of the country's population lived.

Also in July 1990 when the war reached Monrovia, Liberia was cut off from the outside world. The only international airport was Roberts International Airport (Roberts Field) located about thirty miles outside Monrovia near Harbel, and this area was controlled by Taylor, so no flights could come into the country. And Freeport, the port that served Monrovia, was controlled by Prince Johnson, so no ships could come in. The war had disrupted the production of rice in Liberia, so we had become dependent on imported rice. Now the importation of rice stopped.

Those of us who lived in Monrovia, under President Samuel Doe's control, had some money because all the banks were in Monrovia—though most of the banks were looted by Doe's soldiers—but we could not use the money to buy food because the majority of food was in Johnson's Freeport. However, women were sometimes allowed to do business between Monrovia and Freeport. They could cross into Freeport to buy food and return with it to Monrovia. This is how we in Monrovia survived.

Eventually, it became very difficult to find rice, and only soldiers could afford the little rice that there was. Also, food always passed through checkpoints before it reached civilians, so it was available to soldiers first. We civilians ate anything just to survive, such as dog and grass. Sometimes people would eat a plant we called Borbor John. This was a type of grain, but if it was cooked wrong, those who ate it could die—many people died from eating Borbor John. Leaves from hibiscus flowers were also eaten, and almost every coconut tree in Monrovia was cut down for its coconuts.

Often, we lived only on tea and sugar. Sometimes, I gave women what little money I had so they could buy me sugar, milk, and tea bags. Sometimes, I sold a little of my stores just to make sure I didn't run completely out of money. There were times when I received what I sent out for and times I did not. Many times, soldiers took goods from the women before they could get them to me. Soldiers had all the power during the war. They would force us to give them what we had; they might leave us wounded or kill us if we refused.

During this time, an estimated fifty people per day died from malnourishment in Monrovia, and children and the elderly were at the most risk—children were seen throughout the city with bloated bellies from malnourishment and starvation. If the bullets and rockets did not kill, starvation could.

Early in the war, around May or June 1990, the dam that supplied electricity to Liberia was destroyed, so there was no electricity, no running water, and no phone service in the entire country. Only people who could afford to purchase a generator and fuel had power. The destruction of the dam still impacts Liberia because, as of 2017, it has not been repaired.

Many people also died from sickness and disease due to the lack of medicine and medical personnel. The hospitals were closed because many doctors and nurses had fled the country. And many of the doctors and nurses who stayed were killed if they were suspected of supporting one of the rebel groups or were found treating any rebel wounded, or if they were hit by a stray bullet.

The country was a disaster. Many Liberians felt that death was better than life. Thousands did die, and thousands of others fled their homes to escape the fighting. Many ended up in Internally Displaced People (IDP) camps. When a group of displaced people gathered together, this made them an IDP camp in the eyes of the international community. Most people had had to flee their homes quickly, and they arrived at the IDP camps with nothing. Nongovernmental organizations worked to provide these camps with food, water, and medicine. However, in many IDP camps, there was no stable supply of food, no source of safe drinking water, and no medicine.

Many families were separated or torn apart. When rebel or government troops entered a village or an IDP camp, the people would attempt to flee into the surrounding jungle. If caught, fathers were beaten or shot or hacked to death with machetes in front of their wives and children, and mothers and daughters were raped in front of their husbands, fathers, and brothers to spread fear among the civilian population. Young men and children would be forcibly recruited to fight for the rebels or the government.

It took years for many families to be reunited or to find out what happened to their loved ones.

As the bloodshed intensified, there were calls for international intervention. We Liberians hoped the United States would step in. Liberians considered the US to be our father and defender, and we called on them to come and help us, but they said that Liberia was a country of her own making and she should take care of herself, we were an independent nation and they would not interfere in our internal issues. Every nation in the world appeared to turn their backs on Liberia, including the United States.

This was the worst nightmare Liberians could dream. Liberia had always boasted of being a stepchild of the United States, and we believed the US would always be there for us, no matter what. Many other West African nations also believed that the US would come to the aid of Liberia in her time of trouble, but all the US did was evacuate all of their citizens from Liberia, leaving Liberians to their fate.

My job during the war was praying and fasting for my nation and its people. God was the only one we could depend on. We had devotions at the Faulkner's house almost every evening, and many people came to take part. I was the leader for these devotions and ended up becoming well known as a preacher in the community. Many times, soldiers came to me for prayer. Some would tell me to pray that God protect them, and most of them knew me very well. Because I prayed for these soldiers, they called me the Civilian General. God used me in the community so much that, many times, I had soldiers speak up for me when I was in bad situation.

Many of my church brothers and sisters heard about what I was doing in the Buzzie Quarter and decided to come there too. Some of the brothers who had fled Monrovia came back to the area so that we could all live together. The first brother who came to find me in the Buzzie Quarter was Moses Sinyan. Moses was from Grand Bassa County, and he used to be our church drummer when I was a new Christian. I remember I saw him one evening in the

Buzzie Quarter, and I asked him what he was doing back. He said he had heard I was still there, so he came so we could live together at the building we used as our church. This building was very close to my uncle's house.

I still attended African Christian Fellowship International, and Rev. Edward Kofi, the founder and president of ACFI, was my pastor. Our church building was not very big. It was originally a community clinic. Reverend Kofi was a trained nurse and served the community from there. Sometime around 1988, ACFI began holding church services in the clinic. Our church provided medical aid and church services in the Buzzie Quarter, and we received most of our funding from the United States.

Our church had a drug room, infection room, a doctor's office, and a waiting room. The waiting room we used for our services. During the war years, we met there at night to pray and to drink lots of tea. Some soldiers even joined us. There was not much to do during these hard times but pray and struggle together to survive. Whenever there was a cease-fire, some of my friends would leave to search for their families, but I never left the community; I was the Ground Commander. Most of my friends called me by this name because I was always there at the church.

I was spending almost all of my time at the church. Most of the time, I would not even sleep in the new room I had at my Uncle Faulkner's house, because I would sleep at the church. A friend of mine asked me to rent the room at my uncle's to his younger brother, which I did, even though I was paid no rent. This was during the early part of the war, and the fighting had not yet reached Monrovia. When the war got closer to Monrovia, both my friend and his younger brother fled Monrovia and returned to Nimba County, where they were from.

Churches, however, were not always sanctuaries from the war. Doe suspected everyone, and political and religious leaders often went into hiding to escape Doe's death squads. On the night of July 29, 1990, government soldiers entered St. Peter's Lutheran Church on Fourteenth Street in the Sinkor District of Monrovia, where hundreds of displaced people had taken refuge. The soldiers massacred over six hundred men, women, and children. Most of these people were from the Gio and Mano tribes. Among the victims was Nelson Taylor, Charles Taylor's father.

8 ~ GOD SPARES ME

The first rebels to arrest me were from Charles Taylor's NPFL. I believe this happened around August of 1990. My cousin, Wilfred, and I and some of our friends decided to cross the Gabriel Tucker Bridge over the Mesurado River that connects Providence Island to Bushrod Island and Freeport to look for food. Freeport was controlled by Prince Johnson's forces, but his soldiers allowed us to pass. We had been without proper food for more than two weeks, and we were extremely hungry. But there were many people living in Freeport, and we found no food.

Then Wilfred came up with a plan. He told us we could go to an IDP camp at Voice of America (VOA), a radio station set up before the war, in Corma, where his mother had gone for refuge. He told us we could find cassava and other local foods there. We later found out Wilfred was lying to us. He was just trying to find a way to escape from Monrovia to his mother's village, which was very far from the St. Paul Bridge that led north, away from Freeport and Monrovia, and into the territory controlled by Charles Taylor's forces. But we believed Wilfred, and we so badly wanted food, we all decided to go with him.

Wilfred had told us his mother's house was not far from VOA, but he was lying about this as well. We walked about fifteen miles to the VOA camp, and when we arrived, we found the American staff had all left the area and the only people there were a few Liberian refugees. We did not know it, but the area all around VOA was occupied by Charles Taylor's rebels. The refugees at the VOA camp did not tell us the truth about Taylor's troops being nearby. There was only one old man who told us to be very careful and to hurry and leave the area.

We decided to leave the VOA camp, but as we were leaving, we spotted a young man about our age, twenty-six or so. We thought he must be looking for food too, because he was dressed in regular clothes. We had been told Taylor's soldiers all wore American-style uniforms, so we thought nothing of him.

When the man saw us, he called to us, but we paid no attention to him. He demanded we come to him, but we did not. Then he called out for someone to bring him his gun. We realized he had intentionally walked onto the road without his gun so he could spy on travelers. When we heard him call for his gun, we came to our senses and started walking toward him. When his fellow soldiers showed up wearing American-style uniforms, we knew we were in trouble.

This was the first time I had seen Charles Taylor's NPFL. The soldiers detained us and took my watch. They asked our tribe—they were looking for Krahn—and I spoke for all of us and told them we were Kpelle. They asked if any of us were Doe's soldiers. We said no, though one of us was actually a member of the AFL. They searched us and found on the member of the AFL marks on his legs left by the tightly tied high boots worn by the AFL. They accused the man of fighting for Doe, but I tried to assure the soldiers he was no member of the AFL.

Wilfred whispered something into my ear, and I turned around and saw Annette, my former girlfriend from before the war. The NPFL would often capture girls and use them as cooks and sex slaves. Boys were either killed or made into soldiers. These soldiers had captured Annette, and there she was sitting and staring at us, too afraid to speak up for us.

The soldiers ended up releasing us, and Annette told us we should go back to Monrovia quickly because these were bad men. She directed us to the road we should take. Wilfred and one of our friends refused to go back to the city, but the rest of us wanted to get out of that place as fast as possible.

I did not see Wilfred again until 1994.

I never again saw Annette.

We were so scared, we forgot about looking for food and started running for our lives back to Monrovia. On the road, we met a friend of mine, a Gio named Sayee. We felt better when we saw him because he was wearing regular clothing, like the NPFL soldier before, but Sayee was NPFL too. Sayee's attitude was not friendly at all. He asked us where we were going, but when I saw how he was acting toward me, I decided not to tell him the truth—I told him we were seeking refuge in the next town. Sayee also asked if James, my cousin, was still fighting for Doe, but I told him I didn't know. He told me he thought I did know, and he said if he ever saw James he would kill him.

Sayee asked me if I was still living in the Buzzie Quarter, and I told him I was not. He told me he would have shot me if I was still living there. I said, "What?" He said he was just telling me what he would have done if I still lived in the Buzzie Quarter and I was lucky I had left there.

I was shocked that Sayee could act so cruelly toward me. I had been kind to him when we had all lived in the Buzzie Quarter before the war. In fact, I used to help his little brother and let his little brother sleep in my room. When we left Sayee, we were afraid and trembling. When he was out of sight, we again ran for our lives. We ran so much we ended up with sores all between our legs. We made it to the Buzzie Quarter late in the evening and told our story to all of our friends and relatives.

God had spared our lives twice in one day. Where is God in war? Right beside me, where He always is.

After that, I was always afraid to go out and find food, because every time I went, a soldier would trouble me. Sometimes I was forced to carry looted goods for them, and sometimes I was threatened. I decided to not leave the Buzzie Quarter for a time.

During this time, the Liberian people had been repeatedly asking Doe to step down for the good of the country. Our people became so fearful of death at Doe's command, we decided also to appeal to Charles Taylor to put an end to the fighting. He refused. Taylor said he would not give up fighting until Doe surrendered. Doe himself kept telling Taylor and the whole country that he would never surrender to a rebel like Taylor. He would keep fighting until his last soldier was killed. Not even the Liberia Council of Churches, an ecumenical Christian organization founded in Liberia in 1982, could convince Doe and Taylor, the two most powerful factions in the war, to cease the fighting. The Liberia Council of Churches then joined with Muslim leaders and other religious groups to form the Interfaith Mediation Committee and appealed to Doe and Taylor to lay down their weapons. Again, both refused.

There is an African proverb—referenced at one time by Doe himself—*When elephants fight, it is the grass that suffers.* Doe and Taylor were two embattled elephants, and neither would give up the fight at any cost. The helpless people of Liberia were the grass, trampled in the dust and killed in the fighting. The victims of the Liberian Civil War were the Liberian people themselves. This is the truth.

There was now only one being the Liberian people could depend on: God. Liberians all over the country were fasting and praying, asking God to please help us. And God did. He touched the heart of the Nigerian president, Ibrahim Babangida. Babangida made a great financial sacrifice on the part of Nigeria and amassed a fighting force, and he asked all other West African nations to send soldiers and join in coming to the aid of Liberia. As a result, the Economic Community of West African States sent the international peacekeeping force the Economic Community of West African States Monitoring Group (ECOMOG), totaling about four thousand troops, mostly from Nigeria, to Liberia in August 1990.

However, ECOMOG quickly became party to Liberia's homegrown war themselves. Johnson and Doe agreed to allow ECOMOG to enter Liberia, but Taylor was against it. But because Johnson controlled Freeport, the ECOMOG forces were allowed to land there.

Taylor fought fiercely to stop the peacekeepers from landing. It was some of the worst fighting of the war in Monrovia. But even though Taylor sent many of his soldiers, God helped Liberia by giving victory to Prince Johnson and ECOMOG, and the peacekeeping forces entered Liberia.

No Liberian can deny that it was God Himself who helped us that day. We are also grateful to the governments and people of Nigeria, Ghana, Sierra Leonne, Guinea, Senegal, and the other West African nations of the Economic Community of West African States.

After ECOMOG entered Liberia, it set up buffer zones between Johnson and Taylor, between Taylor and Doe, and between Doe and Johnson. Prince Johnson quickly developed close links with ECOMOG. He controlled Freeport, where ECOMOG set up its headquarters, and he frequently visited and socialized with ECOMOG's leaders. In a cease-fire agreement signed on September 5, 1990, Doe agreed not to enter into Johnson's territory without first asking permission.

The three primary warring factions still controlled their territories, but ECOMOG forces were now between them.

However, this was only in Monrovia. ECOMOG did not have enough forces to be present in the entire country—also, Taylor would come against ECOMOG if its soldiers left Monrovia. Taylor was determined to maintain his power and control, so he refused to allow the peacekeepers into the rest of the country.

Many nations continued to ask Doe to step down and leave Liberia. He refused. Many embassies closed their doors, and their personnel left Monrovia while they still could. Only the US embassy remained, with a small staff and a small group of US marines deployed around the embassy compound to keep soldiers from coming in. President Babangida of Nigeria was speaking with other African leaders and the US government to find help for Liberia. He tried to work with other African and world leaders to amass a stronger armed force to bring peace to the entire country. Liberians' hopes now rested on God and the peace talks, but the peace talks failed. They lasted only days before fighting among the factions broke out again.

On September 9, 1990—only four days after the signing of the cease-fire—according to Johnson, Doe decided to visit ECOMOG's headquarters in Freeport without notifying Johnson. The peacekeeping forces required Doe's bodyguards to disarm when they arrived. Johnson heard that Doe was in his territory, and he became very upset that Doe had not asked permission first. Was this true, or was it a trap set up for Doe? We may never know.

Johnson and his men arrived at ECOMOG's headquarters about ten minutes after Doe, but Johnson's men were allowed to keep their weapons. Johnson's men killed most of Doe's unarmed bodyguards and videotaped the torture of Doe. Johnson can be seen in the video drinking a Budweiser as his men cut off Doe's ears. Johnson took one of Doe's ears and ate part of it.

After being tortured for more than a day, Doe was shot dead. His body was placed in a wheelbarrow and paraded around Monrovia. Later, his body was displayed at a medical clinic on Bushrod Island for several days so everyone would know he was dead. Johnson handed out copies of the video documenting the torturing and killing of Doe to the press, ECOMOG leaders, US embassy staff, and leading Monrovian citizens and foes of Doe, including Taylor. But the fighting did not stop simply because Doe was dead. The stakes were too high. Both Prince Johnson and Charles Taylor wanted to be president.

Estimates of the number of people killed up to this point in the war vary from between thirteen thousand and twenty thousand, but I personally believe the total to be much higher. In addition, for ten years as president, Doe had stoked tribal war, and the killings of Mano and Gio tribespeople by Krahn soldiers under his regime led to many revenge killings of Krahn people. By the end of 1990, roughly two-thirds of Liberia's Krahn people had fled the country.

Also under his regime, Doe had elevated the status of the Mandingo people, calling them a *true* Liberian tribe, even though they were no more Liberian than any of the other indigenous tribes, because he wanted their support in the war. As a people, Mandingo were mainly involved in business up until then, but after Doe's endorsement, they became more involved in politics. Doe appointed some Mandingo people to positions in his government, the most famous being Alhaji Kromah, who was made minister of information. Doe and Kromah became very close through their support of one of Liberia's leading soccer clubs, the Mighty Barrolle. Certain people of other tribes resented this attention and came against the Mandingo because they fought alongside Doe. Many Mandingo people also fled Liberia after Doe was killed, fearing for their lives.

However, after Doe was killed, West African leaders were finally able to bring Johnson, Taylor, and other warlords together outside Liberia in Lomé, Togo, for a peace talk. There it was agreed to form an interim government to lead Liberia until elections could be held. This first interim government was headed by Dr. Amos Sawyer, from the Mende tribe, who officially gained authority over most of Monrovia.

Prince Johnson initially supported the Sawyer led government, but Charles Taylor refused to back it and continued the fighting. So ultimately, it failed to lead Liberia to democratic elections and peace. Then Johnson turned against the Sawyer administration for reasons known only to himself and the government. Sawyer had the military support of ECOMOG, and ECOMOG fought Johnson's INPFL and took over Johnson's areas of control in Freeport and on Bushrod Island. Johnson eventually fled to Nigeria in 1992 for refuge from forces supporting Taylor. Some of his INPFL went back to Taylor, and some left Liberia for Guinea and other West African countries.

One day in October 1990, about a month after Doe was killed, we were told Reverend Kofi's wife, Mother Cecelia Kofi, had given birth, and my friends asked me to go with them to see her. At that time, Mother Kofi was living in the Freeport area, in New Kru Town, which was still controlled by Prince Johnson's INPFL, which also controlled the bridge between Monrovia and Bushrod Island. Reverend Kofi and his family used to live in the Sinkor District on Fifth Street but fled their home during the war and moved across the bridge to where Mother Kofi's older brother lived. Reverend Kofi was out of the country at this time, on a mission to the United States to raise funds for the ACFI.

There were many of us living at the ACFI building in the Buzzie Quarter then, and among us were two church sisters named Ellen and Lucia. They used to cross the bridge to Bushrod Island and Freeport to buy fish then return to the Buzzie Quarter to sell it, which they did to help out Mother Kofi, as well as to try to meet their own needs. These ladies did so much for all of us living at the church.

It was because of Ellen and Lucia's encouragement, and because I was the leader of the Buzzie Quarter church and a friend of Mother Kofi's husband, that I finally decided to go with them to see her, even though men were considered threats by all the fighting factions. I was so afraid to make this trip, and I prayed that night for God's protection on us as we traveled across faction lines to see our pastor's wife.

We got up early in the morning to cross the bridge to Bushrod Island. It was very dangerous to travel any time during the day, but Ellen and Lucia knew the right time to go, because they had gone many times to search for food. We left the Buzzie Quarter and crossed the bridge about six thirty, as the sun was rising. When people crossed the bridge to Bushrod Island, INPFL soldiers would order everybody to get into a straight line on the far side so they could inspect each person. The soldiers would send some people to the right and some to the left. If you were sent to the left, it would take a miracle to save you. In line, we had to look straight ahead, or we might be killed. I was terrified.

Most of the fighting groups never treated civilians well. Some even used civilians for target practice. Most young men were forced to fight for one group or another, whether they wanted to or not. To survive the war years, almost all young men, and even little boys and girls, had to be part of a faction. Some joined because they were so disadvantaged and needed food, some because of threats from the factions.

New soldiers might receive only one or two days of training in how to operate an AK-47 rifle and how to maneuver in a combat situation. Younger boys, under eight years old, were used as porters, cooks, launderers, and spies. As spies, young boys would go into a village ahead of the troops and report back what they saw. This job was very dangerous. Young girls were also used as porters, cooks, and launderers. But older girls often became sex slaves for the soldiers, and some were given away to soldiers as wives. Some older girls, however, became soldiers themselves.

Even though the Liberian Civil War ended in 2003, the boys and girls recruited during the war still live with many traumas.

When I was in line on the far side of the bridge, the INPFL soldiers told me to go to the left. One soldier declared I was an enemy to them. He told me to take off all my clothes. All I was allowed to keep on was my underwear. All of my friends started to cry and plead for my release, but the soldier said he was taking me to the river to kill me. He made me walk in front of him to the river with his rifle pointed at my head.

I walked toward the river. Then I saw a man sitting on a porch railing, and the soldier told the man I was an enemy and he was going to kill me. I did not know this man who was sitting on the railing, but he spoke right up to the soldier and said I was not an enemy, I was not of the Krahn tribe, as the soldier supposed. After that, the soldier lowered his weapon. I remember telling the soldier I was never going to be a part of any faction. He told me I was very lucky and I was the only person he had ever brought to the river and not killed.

After the soldier said this, I looked around, but I did not see the man who had had the courage to speak up for my release. There was no one there but the soldier and myself. I only remember that the man had been wearing a white, long-sleeved shirt and had been sitting on the railing of a porch. I believe God sent an angel to save me from being killed that day. The soldier told me to go then turned and walked away toward the main road and the bridge.

There I was, alone, practically naked, and very confused. I don't know how long I stood there, not far from the river, but when I realized the soldier was walking away, I finally came to myself and slowly followed behind him. When I returned to the main road, I saw many people watching me. My friend, Moses, and another church sister were still standing near the bridge crying; Ellen and Lucia had gone to appeal to one of the rebel commanders on my behalf. When my friends saw me coming back, Moses ran to me and held me in his arms, and our sister began to sing praise songs to God because He had spared my life.

Everyone still standing in line who knew the soldier who had taken me to the river said it was the first time this man had allowed someone to come back alive. They said I was so very lucky, but I told them I had been spared by God. I asked Moses where Ellen and Lucia were, and he told me they had gone to Prince Johnson's base, about ten miles from where we were at the bridge, to plead for my release. Moses and I decided to go look for them and then saw Ellen coming back in our direction. When Ellen saw me, she could not believe it and started crying.

We had to run after Lucia. Ellen told us Lucia had gone to tell Mother Kofi and the others that I had been arrested and killed. By the grace of God, we found her before she got to Mother Kofi's.

Moses saw Lucia first, near a place called Point Four in New Kru Town, and yelled her name in the midst of a huge crowd—it was the main market area of the town. Lucia turned and saw us then ran toward us in tears. She ran to me and hugged me. Lucia had been so confused and upset when I was arrested, she had dropped the clothes, baby supplies, and other items she had been bringing to Mother Kofi. She wanted to go and look for these things, but we told her to just forget about them because someone must have taken them by that time.

So we went on our way to see Mother Kofi.

When we arrived at the place where Mother Kofi was staying, we found that she had gone to take a bath. We were allowed to enter the room where she and her children lived, and we saw her children, including the newborn baby. I took the baby girl in my arms and heard Lucia talking to her in Liberian English, telling her this man holding her was almost killed on his way to meet her. Poor child—what did she know about war?

In a little while, Mother Kofi came out of the bathroom, so Moses and I went out so she would have some privacy. Later on, we were called inside and found that Lucia and Ellen had already started to explain what had happened. We spent some time visiting with Mother Kofi and the children then decided to head back to the Buzzie Quarter. Mother Kofi wanted us to spend the night, but I refused because I was afraid it was too dangerous. So we went shopping and bought our usual food items—tea bags, milk, sugar, fish, and whatever else we could buy in Freeport—then headed for the bridge.

When we arrived at the bridge, we could not cross. A whole crowd was waiting for someone to be the first to step out onto the bridge. The bridge was no-man's-land. It separated Doe's former AFL soldiers on the Monrovia side from Prince Johnson's INPFL on the Bushrod side, and everyone there was too afraid to be the first to try to cross.

Some of our friends were waiting with the crowd at the bridge, and they told us to wait until Johnson's men gave us the go ahead. But I knew this was a bad place for me, and I wanted to get across as soon as I could. I did not want the man who had wanted to kill me to see me again. Everybody told me not to cross, but I refused to listen to them. I grabbed my backpack and started walking toward the bridge. I said to myself, "If I am going to get shot, that's it, but I cannot spend one more minute standing at this dangerous place." I thought of the Liberian proverb: *He who has a downfall fears no evil.* I felt I had already been in the middle of the river, so why should I be afraid of drowning?

I was praising God in my heart, and I walked all the way to the middle of the bridge before I turned my head to look back, and when I did, the entire crowd was behind me, Moses, Lucia, Ellen, and everyone.

That day, a dead man became a hero. People told me I was too brave. But I was not brave; I only did what I had to do. I knew what I had been through with the soldier who had wanted to kill me. This was the place where he had arrested me, so standing around wasting time at that same place meant looking for more trouble. Every time I remember this story, I am so thankful to God.

9 ~ REBECCA

On November 27, 1990, another peace agreement—one of many during the war—was signed in Mali. This agreement established a cease-fire, allowed humanitarian aid to enter Monrovia, and created an interim government—Amos Sawyer was sworn in as Liberia's interim president. Taylor and his NPFL controlled roughly 90 percent of Liberia at this time, while the late Doe's AFL and Prince Johnson's INPFL continued to control the areas in and around Monrovia.

Fighting between the three major factions started up again soon after the November agreement was signed, and representatives met again in Lomé in February 1991 and signed yet another peace agreement. This peace agreement established a timetable for disarmament, and there were meetings in Monrovia in March and April to work out the details of the disarmament, but the agreement fell apart when Taylor insisted that he be given the presidency.

On March 23, 1991, a group calling itself the Revolutionary United Front (RUF) invaded Sierra Leone from Liberia. The RUF was led by Foday Sankoh, who was born and raised in Sierra Leone and had been a corporal in the army there, but he had taken part in a mutiny and was sent to prison. After Sankoh was released from prison, he joined a rebel group that traveled to Libya, where he received military training and met Charles Taylor. He joined forces with Taylor and fought for him during the early part of the Liberian Civil War.

Taylor and the NPFL supplied funding, weapons, and many of the troops for Sankoh's invasion of Sierra Leone. Sankoh's goal was to capture and control key locations of Sierra Leone's diamond trade. Horror is the best word to describe the war that Charles Taylor helped to start in Sierra Leone. He would eventually be tried and convicted of crimes against humanity by the World Court in the Hague for what he caused in that country.

In May 1991, yet another faction appeared to trouble Liberia. The United Liberation Movement of Liberia for Democracy (ULIMO) was formed by three former Doe supporters in Sierra Leone after they had fled to that country following Doe's death. Alhaji Kromah, Doe's former minister of information, was joined by Albert Karpeh and George Boley, both Krahn tribesmen and former members of Doe's cabinet. The sole stated purpose of the ULIMO was to fight back against Taylor. The government of Sierra Leone wanted to put pressure on Taylor for his part in the fighting there, so they allowed the ULIMO to operate out of Sierra Leone.

The ULIMO joined forces with the Sierra Leonean Army and the West African peacekeeping forces of ECOMOG and fought the combined forces of Sankoh and Taylor—the RUF and the NPFL. Eventually, after the RUF and NPFL were pushed out of Sierra Leonne, Kromah's ULIMO was able to invade western Liberia from Sierra Leonne with about three thousand troops in September 1991. They fought Taylor's forces there and gained territory in counties Lofa and Bomi.

In 1991, beginning in June and ending in October, another peace conference headed by Nigeria convened in the Ivory Coast. A very complex agreement was reached calling for a cease-fire, the creation of a buffer zone between Liberia and Sierra Leonne, a new interim government for Liberia, and disarmament of the warring factions. Taylor supported this agreement, because it provided his forces some relief from the attacks of the ULIMO.

This cease-fire lasted until October 1992, when Charles Taylor invaded Monrovia. Taylor called this invasion Operation Octopus. ECOMOG forces were on the verge of being overrun, so they had to rearm the AFL, whose members had been confined to their barracks in Monrovia since 1990 for fear they would rejoin the fighting, and enlist the help of the ULIMO. ECOMOG also used aircraft, naval guns, and artillery to bomb and shell the NPFL controlled areas of Monrovia. An estimated 6,500 civilians died during this battle, which lasted through November 1992. Taylor was eventually pushed out of Monrovia and lost control of almost half of his territory.

Fighting continued for several months in the rural areas of Liberia, forcing Taylor to return to the peace table. Another cease-fire was called. The United Nations reported that by July 1993, 150,000 Liberians had lost their lives since the war started in 1989 and 700,000 Liberians (35 percent of the population) were refugees. Personally, I believe these estimated numbers were low.

Whenever there was a cease-fire between the factions, we had some freedom to move between communities. For example, the Buzzie Quarter was, for a long time, controlled by Doe's AFL, so I could move between other areas under its control without the risk of being killed. It was still not safe, however, to move between areas that were controlled by other factions. You could get killed going where nobody knew you, as I was almost killed crossing the bridge to Bushrod Island. Some people still took the chance and went to other areas of Monrovia under different control, but they were gambling with their lives. Some of those who did cross faction lines lived, others died.

During these times of cease-fire, I always went with a group of pastors and evangelists, including Moses, James Kollie, and Pastor Dennis Gaye, out to do street preaching and community outreach, or crusades, which made me popular among different communities. When we preached, we spoke of forgiveness and reconciliation. At this time in Liberia, there was a lot of hatred and unforgiveness between tribes and communities and among the people in general. This was due to the increasingly ethnic character of the violence. We tried to teach people forgiveness is good for the soul.

We taught that we live in a fallen world filled with fallen and imperfect people. It is not a question of who has been hurt, it is a question of who needs to be set free. Sometimes we excuse our lack of forgiveness on the grounds the one who has wronged us does not deserve our forgiveness. But the problem with this view is no one has ever wronged us as we have wronged God. When we accept God's grace, it comes into our hearts and makes us forgiving. If we are refusing to forgive, we should look into our hearts and see if we have been forgiven. Each of us needs to learn to forgive because of what Jesus Christ has done for us.

It was during one of our crusades I met my future wife, Rebecca.

Before we met, Rebecca Warner and her family had attempted to move from Bassa Community in Monrovia, which was controlled by Doe at the time, to Paynesville, which is in southeastern Monrovia and was controlled by Taylor. Like so many others, they believed the promises they heard that they would be safer under Taylor.

A story had been circulating that Taylor was asking people to leave Doe's control areas in Monrovia and promising not to kill anyone who did. Taylor's men told people there was food and safety under Taylor. All this was lies. In truth, Taylor's men killed anyone they thought had been a Doe supporter. It was likely someone might be killed just because he came from an area controlled by Doe.

This is how Rebecca lost her father.

Rebecca's father, Mr. Warner, believing the false promises of Taylor and his men, decided to move his family from Bassa Community to Paynesville. Mr. Warner had been a military man in the AFL long before Doe had ever come to power. When the Warner's attempted to cross faction lines, Taylor's men identified Mr. Warner as former AFL, and from that point, he was a marked man. Taylor's soldiers rounded up the family and separated Mr. Warner and his son, Maxwell, from Mrs. Nora Warner and the two girls, Rebecca and Phermar. The soldiers took Nora, Rebecca, and Phermar, in a different direction from Mr. Warner and Maxwell, so they did not witness what happened.

Taylor's men killed Mr. Warner right in front of Maxwell, and it was many months before Maxwell was able to get back to his family and confirm what they had been hearing: their husband and father was dead.

After Maxwell was able to rejoin his family, Nora decided to return with her children to Bassa Community. They returned to their house to find it had been looted, but they settled down and started finding the means to survive. Nora was a midwife, so this helped a little. She was called Ma Nora, and she was very helpful to pregnant women in Bassa Community and surrounding communities.

During one of the cease-fires, we held a three-evening crusade in Bassa Community, and Nora came the first evening. After the first evening came to a close, we were picking up our instruments and equipment to take with us back to our church in the Buzzie Quarter, and Nora came up to us. She offered us water and told us we could store our instruments and equipment at her home, as we were going to be in Bassa Community again the next two evenings. And we decided it would be good to not have to carry our instruments and equipment from the Buzzie Quarter to Bassa Community each evening.

That first night, Nora told us her story and asked us to pray for her and her children, who were not home that evening, and she promised to bring them to the crusade the next two evenings. When I went to say goodnight to her on that first night, Nora told me again how she wanted her children to take part in the crusade, and while we were chatting, Rebecca, Phermar, and Maxwell came home, and Nora introduced me to them. We talked a little while longer, and then I left for home.

During the second evening of the crusade, Rebecca was among those who accepted Jesus Christ as their Lord and Savior. After the service, we always held a follow-up so these new Christians could receive encouragement to begin active Christian living and knowing God better through prayer, Bible study, discipleship, and ministry. We invited them to our church or made sure they knew about a church in their area. Rebecca became part of our little church in the Buzzie Quarter, and she was very committed to attending wherever we held a crusade. She has a very good voice, and sometimes she sang with us. After a year or so, we started dating.

There are many reasons I was drawn to Rebecca. She is beautiful, determined, and very serious about her relationship with Christ. She is also very truthful about herself. And she, like me, had lived with different family members who were not her biological parents. Nora was not her birth mother, but Rebecca lived with her from the time she was a child until we were married. Rebecca's birth parents lived in a very rural area of Bong County. They sent their children to live with the Warner's because they were too poor to care for them or provide them an education. Rebecca is a very caring, hard-working, and loving woman. I am blessed to have her as my wife.

My late mentor, Pastor Dennis Gaye, played a very important role in my and Rebecca's relationship. Dating was a major step for us. Pastor Gaye taught us dating was a time of getting to know one another well, without the physical aspects of a relationship, and Rebecca and I spent much time with him studying the Word of God and learning God's intentions for marriage. Pastor Gaye told us we were not allowed to kiss or even be alone together before we were married. I found these rules very hard to follow, but by the special grace of God, we did follow them.

One heartbreaking aspect of my and Rebecca's wedding was our biological parents were not able to be present, in part because it would have been too dangerous for them to travel to Monrovia. Also, there was no reliable means of communication in Liberia during this time, so we were unable to even send our parents news of our upcoming marriage. While we were happy about our union, we were also sad about not being able to have our parents there for such a special event. We talked about it often and prayed God would grant we find our parents alive when the fighting finally ended. And by the grace of God, we were both able to see our parents again. God is good.

Rebecca and I were married on March 12, 1994, in the Sinkor District of Monrovia at the ACFI headquarters church, Ocean View Chapel. The wedding went well, even though we had to be very cautious of the ongoing fighting. Rev. Edward Kofi, Pastor Dennis Gaye, and several other pastors officiated at our wedding. Timing was very important, because there was a seven to seven curfew in place. The entire wedding ceremony and reception needed to be over before six in the evening to give our friends and relatives more time to get home before the curfew.

After the wedding ceremony, Rebecca and I left the church for a short ride to take our wedding photo while organizers prepared the church for a short reception. We did not have much to offer, but people were served from the little provided by Reverend Kofi and members of our church family.

Up to this time, I had not found a place to live with Rebecca. I paid for a room on Camp Johnson Road, right outside the Buzzie Quarter, but the room owner lied to me and stole my money—he rented the room to both me and another person, and the other person took the room first. We did not cancel the wedding, because I still had faith the Lord would help us find a place to live. But I was still looking for a place the very day of the wedding.

During the reception, however, Reverend Kofi told me he had found a room for me and Rebecca to live in for two weeks in a house close to the ACFI headquarters that was owned by one of his friends. God is good.

After the wedding, Reverend Kofi left for the United States. He would be back in two weeks with guests and was planning to have them stay in the room Rebecca and I now occupied. We tried to find another place to live, but we found nothing. When Reverend

Kofi was told we had been unable to find another place to live and were still in the room, he made a call and arranged for me and Rebecca to take a room at the ACFI headquarters until we could find somewhere else to live. And so at the end of the two weeks, we moved into the ACFI headquarters. The ACFI headquarters are right on the Atlantic Ocean. Ocean View Chapel and three houses are located on the property.

Also before the wedding, I was not working, but when Reverend Kofi returned from his trip to the US, he offered me a job. He told me he had decided Rebecca and I should stay at the ACFI headquarters and I should serve as director for the church grounds. He also asked me to help take care of his children and the other children who were living there with him. Surely, God is good!

I started out earning five hundred Liberian dollars, which was about five to seven US dollars, per month. I was very happy about this. And after a few weeks, Reverend Kofi increased my pay to eight hundred Liberian dollars, which was about eight to ten US dollars. Offering me and Rebecca a place to live plus ten dollars per month was a great blessing to us, especially because so many Liberians were out of work due to the war. Because of my job, Rebecca and I also received food. I took care of feeding the Kofi's children, and we shared in the food. Blessings, blessings from the Lord.

I continued to work for ACFI, and Rebecca and I lived at the ACFI headquarters from after we were married in 1994 until the start of the terrible fighting in Monrovia on April 6, 1996.

Rebecca was twenty-one years old when we were married and in eleventh grade. We had to keep our wedding a secret from Rebecca's school administrators and teachers, because at that time, a married person was not allowed to attend morning school in Liberia. Morning school was for young people, not married people. If Rebecca's school administrators had found out she was married, she would have been expelled.

Some of Rebecca's school mates knew about our wedding, but they helped keep it secret, and Rebecca never wore her wedding ring to school. Mercifully, the school year was almost over when we were married, and by God's grace, the school year came to an end and Rebecca was promoted to the senior class.

However, we did have a surprise before Rebecca was able to finish school: Rebecca became pregnant.

At first, Rebecca and I did not know she was pregnant. One day toward the end of the 1994 school year, Rebecca had gone to school and felt sick, so she went by Nora's after school to rest. Ma Nora was experienced, and when she looked at Rebecca, she knew her daughter was pregnant.

I remember sitting out on the front porch of the ACFI building where we now lived waiting for Rebecca to come home from school. Instead, I saw her younger sister, Phermar, coming toward me. I hurriedly went toward her and asked why she had come. She told me, "Your wife is unwell at our house, and Ma sent me to call you." I went with her quickly to find Rebecca.

At Nora's house, I asked Nora what was making Rebecca sick, and her response was, "You know what is making her sick." I asked what she meant, and she said, "I think she's pregnant."

Nora was angry with me because Rebecca was pregnant and her plan for Rebecca was not to become pregnant until she completed high school. Nora said to me, "This is the reason I did not want you two to get married, because I wanted my daughter to complete high school before getting pregnant, but now see what you have done!"

While Nora was lashing her anger at me, Rebecca was crying. I was so embarrassed, I did not know what to say to Rebecca or Nora. When Rebecca realized I was embarrassed and feeling ashamed in front of her mother, she told Nora she wanted to go with me so I could take her to a medical clinic in the Sinkor District, close to where we now lived. We went straight to the clinic to find out if what Nora was saying was true. At the clinic, the nurse told us it was true, Rebecca was pregnant. The nurse asked what we wanted to do, if we wanted to keep the child or abort it. We both said, in very strong tones, "No abortion."

After we left the clinic, I do not know how to describe my emotions at realizing Rebecca's pregnancy. It was the best news I could imagine, even though Nora was furious with us. It was a blessing from the Lord, and that day became such a beautiful day.

On November 29, 1994, Rebecca gave birth to our oldest son, Joshua Shadrach Kwalalon.

When Rebecca went into labor, I dropped her off at the John F. Kennedy (JFK) Medical Center in the Sinkor District, which at the time was controlled by the AFL. I was so afraid. I did not stay with my wife during the delivery of our son, because I felt I knew nothing about what was about to happen. I left the hospital and went home. I prayed for my wife and my child being born and only went back to the hospital when I was sent news my wife had given birth to a bouncing baby boy.

I named our firstborn Joshua for two reasons: The first reason is an American missionary's son asked me to. The boy's family had come to Liberia on a mission trip. He was only six or seven years old, and his name was Josh. Rebecca was pregnant at the time, and the little boy asked me to name our unborn child Josh if it was a boy and after Abraham's wife, Sarah, if it was a girl. I promised to do just that. The second reason is biblical names are very important to me, and Joshua from the Old Testament happens to be one of my biblical heroes.

God is good.

All through this time, Liberia had no peace. On March 7, 1994, a few days before Rebecca and I were married, the Sawyer-led interim government was replaced by a council of state, headed by David Kpormakpor, to fulfill a peace agreement signed in July 1993. The Liberian Council of State was set up by the Economic Community of West African States and backed by the United States. Kpormakpor was born in 1944 in rural Liberia and was considered a *bush boy*, having been raised by Gola parents who could neither read nor write. However, a missionary decided Kpormakpor had potential, so he secured a scholarship for Kpormakpor to attend school in Monrovia. After Kpormakpor graduated from high school, he won scholarships to San Francisco State University and, later, to UCLA Law School. He returned home, became a professor of law, and was eventually appointed to the Liberian Supreme Court by President Samuel Doe.

As interim president between 1994 and 1995, Kpormakpor had little power but access to millions of government dollars. While many of his colleagues plundered government funds, Kpormakpor continued to claim he maintained a reputation as the only honest politician in Liberia. Others called him a fool.

The Liberian Council of State included members from each of the major warring factions. This was done in an effort to stop the fighting. However, the fighting continued, with even more factions appearing and fighting to gain territory and power. The ULIMO, which had been having internal problems from its beginning in 1991, finally split into two separate factions, the ULIMO-J and the

ULIMO-K, early in 1994.

The split in the ULIMO occurred when the Krahn leader, Albert Karpeh, was murdered by a group of Mandingo soldiers under the command of Alhaji Kromah. The Krahns left the ULIMO and formed their own fighting group led by Roosevelt Johnson, which they called the ULIMO-Johnson (ULIMO-J). Johnson was Krahn and had been a teacher before the war. He had also been targeted for death by Kromah, because he was one of Karpeh's chief officers, but he escaped. The remaining ULIMO soldiers loyal to Alhaji Kromah were now primarily Mandingo and became the ULIMO-Kromah (ULIMO-K). So now there was the ULIMO-J and the ULIMO-K, and both factions swapped alliances with other factions frequently. They fought against Charles Taylor, and they fought against each other.

George Boley, the third founder of the original ULIMO, had split from the group in 1993 and formed the Liberia Peace Council.

Every faction controlled certain territory and looted its resources. Factions sometimes traded looted goods with each other, making alliances that lasted for a time then broke apart. The soldiers of the Economic Community of West African States Monitoring Group were supposed to be our peacekeepers. But they could not be trusted either. They looted and traded with and took payments from the factions. A saying began in Liberia that ECOMOG stood for Every Car Or Movable Object Gone.

Some of the counties and tribes decided to form defense forces to protect their own people. Politicians formed their own small factions so they might be included in the interim government.

There was confusion everywhere.

And it was a time of evil in the highest forms—witchcraft, cannibalism, not to mention random killings. You could be walking down the street with a friend, and a soldier might tell you to stop and simply kill one of you.

Then in August 1994, another peace agreement was signed that was again supposed to lead to disarmament. This agreement was signed in Abuja, Nigeria, and included a new Council of State of Liberia made up again of major faction leaders and other well-known Liberians. The council members were: Wilton Sankawolo, chairman, an educator and writer who served in the Tubman, Tolbert, and Doe administrations; Charles Taylor, the head of the National Patriotic Front of Liberia and the most powerful faction leader; Alhaji Kromah, the leader of the ULIMO-K; George Boley, the leader of the Liberia Peace Council; Chief Tamba Taylor, a well-known chief of the Kissi people; and Oscar Quiah, the minister of internal affairs in the Doe administration. Leaders from lesser factions were appointed to lower government positions. Roosevelt Johnson, for example, was named a minister, as the ULIMO-J did not yet hold much power. All government leaders kept offices in Monrovia.

There was some small movement toward peace and security after this most recent peace agreement was signed, but when the disarmament process started, it was estimated there were about 60,000 combatants fighting across Liberia, and by August 24, 1994, only 3,612 combatants had been disarmed. Fighting soon broke out again.

In September 1994, General Julu, who led the Liberian Army in the raids in Nimba County during the Doe presidency, gathered three hundred former Liberian Army soldiers and took over the Executive Mansion, declaring himself president of Liberia. ECOMOG forces retook control of the Executive Mansion the following day.

Later in September, a trio of NPFL members, including Samuel Dokie, broke with Taylor and formed their own faction called the Central Revolutionary Council of the National Patriotic Front of Liberia (CRC-NPFL), and they gathered enough soldiers to drive Taylor from his stronghold in Gbarnga.

Near the end of 1994, when our son Joshua was born, there were at least seven major factions fighting to control various parts of Liberia. And these groups were constantly re-allying themselves with each other. Often the fighting appeared to be completely ethnic in nature, with one tribe fighting another. But regardless of the reasons for the fighting, one thing was clear: it was a seemingly endless cycle of brutal violence.

Finally, on August 19, 1995, yet another peace agreement was signed—at least ten peace agreements were signed before this. This agreement called for a cease-fire, effective August 26, 1995, the formation of a new council of state, the deployment of ECOMOG and UN forces throughout Liberia, and disarmament, occurring between January 1 and January 31, 1996.

The new council of state was made up of three men from the most powerful factions, Charles Taylor (NPFL), Alhaji Kromah

(ULIMO-K), and George Boley (Liberia Peace Council), and three civilians, Tamba Taylor, Oscar Quiah, and Wilton Sankawolo, who was again named chairman. The civilian members had no military backing, so they were fairly ineffectual in the peace process. Leaders of the four smaller major factions were again given lesser government positions.

On August 31, 1995, Monrovians lined the streets for nine miles leading to the Executive Mansion to witness Charles Taylor entering the city. Taylor was dressed in all white and drove his own car through the city. We believed true peace had finally arrived. On September 1, 1995, the new Council of State of Liberia was installed.

The peace agreement of August 19, 1995, lasted about two weeks before heavy fighting broke out again in the rural areas. The council of state could not work together because each of the faction leaders wanted all the power for himself.

And Liberia drifted back toward anarchy.

10 ~ 1996: WAR IS HELL

In February 1996 for reasons best known to himself, Charles Taylor demanded Roosevelt Johnson of ULIMO-J be arrested. Johnson told the government leadership he would never allow Charles Taylor to have him arrested, and he took a complaint to the Interfaith Mediation Committee and asked them to advise Taylor to stop pursuing him. Leaders of the Interfaith Mediation Committee tried to advise Taylor against arresting Johnson, but Taylor refused to listen. Johnson then appealed to the Liberian people to stop Taylor, but nobody could, because Taylor's military force was the largest among the factions. Also, many Liberians did not understand what Johnson had done to make Taylor want to arrest him. Johnson finally told the council of state and the Liberian people if Taylor tried to force his arrest, it could lead again to full-scale war.

Not everyone on the council of state agreed with Taylor, but he tried to convince them with accusations that Johnson's ULIMO-J had killed one of his men. Chairman Sankawolo, for his part, said nothing to defend Johnson and agreed with Taylor to have Johnson arrested. Taylor had influence over Sankawolo, because Sankawolo commanded no army, and when the new wave of fighting started, Taylor moved Sankawolo to the Taylor home in Congo Town, about ten miles southeast of Monrovia.

On April 5, 1996, Charles Taylor gathered his NPFL from all his control areas in Liberia to launch a forceful arrest of Roosevelt Johnson in Monrovia. Taylor told his fellow state council members it would be a matter of no more than one day to have Johnson arrested and brought to justice.

They all forgot or ignored Johnson's promise of full-scale resistance.

It was early on the morning of April 6 that Taylor ordered his NPFL to move in and arrest Johnson. Johnson had been living on

Nineteenth Street in the Sinkor District, but when Taylor's forces attacked, he retreated into the barracks of the Barclay Training Center. These barracks were built by the Tubman administration to protect the Executive Mansion and were formidable. The barracks were mainly occupied by Krahn at the time, and most of the Krahn fought for Johnson's ULIMO-J and were willing to give their lives in support of their leader. What Taylor and his supporters thought would be a simple arrest became anything but.

This was the beginning of the worst fighting of the war so far in Monrovia, and Liberia as a whole. Houses and businesses were looted and burned in Monrovia by fighters from all factions, and many fighters and innocent people were killed.

Alhaji Kromah and his ULIMO-K joined forces with Taylor's NPFL to fight Johnson, and both factions began referring to their fighters as government forces. The ECOMOG peace keepers withdrew and did nothing to protect the civilian population. However, they cannot truly be blamed—they were far outnumbered and took refuge from the fighting themselves.

At the time, I was still working for ACFI, and Rebecca and I were still living at the headquarters in the Sinkor District with Joshua. My friend, Thomas Peters, and I were in charge of mission activities. ACFI had just received some humanitarian-relief containers. They were sent by Christian Aid Ministries and included rice, corn oil, sugar, flour, beans, milk, vitamins, and medicine. These supplies would help feed and provide for the nine orphans and eight blind men we housed at the ACFI headquarters at the time. The orphans had all lost their parents during the fighting—many were from outlying villages. The blind men were all in their twenties and from the community and were completely dependent on us as well.

Before the fighting, on March 31, I was visited by my sister Marion and asked to find all means possible to return to Yowee. My brother, John, had been stopped by some of Taylor's soldiers, for some unknown reason, and beaten severely. Some people who knew him and our family sent a message to our parents. My father and some of our relatives went to find him, but by the time they arrived, he was almost at the point of death. They decided to carry him back to Yowee, but while they were still on the way, John bled to death.

My parents asked me to return to Yowee to see where John was buried and to take my two younger brothers, Alex, sixteen, and Lawrence, twelve, out of the village and back to Monrovia. Gbarnga had once again become Charles Taylor's stronghold, and Yowee being so close to Gbarnga meant constant threats, which still included young boys being forcefully recruited into the NPFL or other factions, and my parents did not want my brothers to be caught up in the fighting.

On April 1, Marion and I left Monrovia for Yowee, but I would need to be back before April 6, a Saturday, so I could take part in a church brother and sister's wedding. We were driven to Foequelleh by one of my aunty's sons (the aunty who mistreated me), Gaye, who was a fighter in Taylor's NPFL and was well known in Taylor's control areas. Gaye dropped us off in Foequelleh in the evening, and asked another NPFL soldier to give us a place to spend the night so we could start on foot for Yowee in the morning. The man showed us where we could sleep, but I felt he looked dangerous, and I did not trust him, so I told my sister we would not be spending the night there. We would walk all night to Yowee.

There was another family in Foequelleh travelling to their home village of Balakoah, located just before Yowee. They were also afraid to stay the night, so I said we should travel together and leave at once. The family agreed. But Marion and I were afraid to tell the soldier who was providing us a place to sleep we would not be staying. So I went to him and told him I was going to look for a friend of my father's, but I lied to him. He told me we could go to the room he had shown us earlier whenever we were ready to sleep, but he said he would not be sleeping because he had to go on guard duty. I was so glad to hear that, and I said I would see him in the morning. I returned to my sister and the family headed for Balakoah and told everyone we must leave, so we started walking. It was already dark.

We walked the whole night and arrived at Balakoah early the next morning. The family took us to their home and gave us water to wash our faces. I did not want to spend much time there, because Yowee was still some distance away. They wanted us to wait so they could find food for us, because we had had nothing to eat all night, but I insisted Marion and I were fine and needed to get going right away. It was daytime and my father was well known in the area because my grandfather had been a tribal chief, so I felt better about the rest of our walk to Yowee.

We walked the whole morning and reached Yowee in the early afternoon. It was an emotional reunion with my family because of the loss of my brother. It was difficult to tell my parents I needed to be back in Monrovia before Saturday for the wedding and I could not stay long. However, I was able to spend nearly two days grieving with them.

There was more food in Yowee than there was in Monrovia, so my family wanted us to take some back to the city with us. But we could not, because we had to walk quite a distance before we could hire a car to take us the rest of the way to Monrovia. To solve this problem, my father decided to ask some of our relatives to carry food ahead of us to Foequelleh, where we would try to find a car. Early on the morning of April 4, Alex and Lawrence, my two younger brothers, and some men left to carry our food to Foequelleh, and I stayed in Yowee with my parents to grieve and rest for the journey the next day.

But late that night, my brothers and the men came back still carrying some of the food. They told us on the way to Foequelleh, there were soldiers from the NPFL forcing young men to join up, so they dropped some of what they were carrying and ran into the jungle to escape being captured. The trail to Foequelleh was no longer an option, so what could we do? I asked my parents to show us another way to Monrovia. The route they showed us went through Janapleta and involved five times more walking than the original route, but I said we would take it.

Fortunately, my brothers and an aunty (the half-sister of my mother) who was accompanying us back to Monrovia knew this route. I decided we could not spend the night in Yowee, so my brothers, my sister, my aunty, and I started out around eleven and walked all through the night. We walked all morning and into the afternoon, and finally, we arrived in Janapleta around three.

To hire a car to travel during this time was very difficult. Almost all cars belonged to soldiers. While we were waiting for a car, we were so hungry I asked Marion and our aunty to cook some food for us. They cooked some rice, and while we were eating, a van driven by a soldier showed up. The van only had seats left for three people, and we were five. The driver was a general in Taylor's NPFL. I asked him if all five of us could travel, and he told me if some of us could sit on laps, we could come.

We climbed into the van with our food in our hands. It took a long time to travel from Janapleta to Gbarnga because there were so many checkpoints—at every checkpoint, we all had to step out of the van and the general who was our driver had to spend money to raise the gate. Checkpoint fees were required of everyone except Taylor's most highly ranked men, and the general driving us was not one of these.

Finally, we pulled into Gbarnga. The usual time for this drive would have been about an hour, but because of all the checkpoints, it took us more than five. Then we spent time in Gbarnga looking for other passengers to fill the van. We left for the remaining 120-mile trip to Monrovia around nine at night, and we got close to Kakata, which is about fifty miles from Monrovia, around midnight, but were told not to go into town because it was not safe at that hour.

The general took all of us in the van to an abandoned house to give us a place to rest. The women slept in the house, and all the men stayed outside to keep watch. That general was friendly with me and allowed me to stay close to him. He asked me to walk with him to another checkpoint so we could find out about the situation in Kakata, but I was too afraid because I was not a soldier. So I told him I was too tired and wanted to take a little sleep. He told me to sit in the van and sleep small (a little while) while he went with some NPFL soldiers to see his friends at the next checkpoint.

After an hour, he returned and told us he had learned Taylor was planning to move on Monrovia and take it over. We called together everyone who had been traveling in the van and told them to get ready to leave for Kakata. Things were becoming very dangerous in the area, and the general thought Kakata would be the best place for us because there were still some ECOMOG peace keepers there. He planned to turn us over to the ECOMOG soldiers, and as civilians, we should be safe.

When we got to Kakata early that morning, we were in for an unpleasant surprise. Things were tense there. The NPFL had arrested all the peacekeepers and disarmed them. We were told that we were on our own, and the general turned all of us over to the NPFL. We were given no place to rest and were told we had to wait until the soldiers received news that the road to Monrovia was clear so we could travel. We spent the entire night next to a building that Taylor's troops were using as a police station. Early the next morning, a soldier told us that the road to Monrovia was still unsafe, but we decided to leave anyway.

Around noon, my brothers, sister, aunty, and I made it to an area southeast of Monrovia called Red Light, where two main roads intersect—before the war, the intersection had a traffic light, and because traffic lights are not common in Liberia, the area was named for it. While we were looking for a taxi, I saw my friend, Thomas Peters, driving Reverend Kofi's car. Peters was trying to find a way to get to Reverend Kofi's mother. She was trapped on Twenty-Fourth Street in the Sinkor District with some of her children and grandchildren. Peters could not get to her because of the fighting in the area.

Peters told me it was impossible for him to get through to Ma Kofi from where we were, so we all got into the car with him to try to find another way. We left all of the food we had brought from Yowee with a friend with the intention of coming back to get it. We decided to drive east then north and west to cross over Bushrod Island to downtown Monrovia—all of this territory was controlled by Taylor's NPFL and the interim government—to approach the Sinkor District. We finally arrived in the Sinkor District on the morning of April 6 and met Reverend Kofi and some of the church members who had come to the ACFI headquarters to receive food from the delivery from Christian Aid Ministries and to seek refuge.

Many people in Monrovia were at first trying to ignore the fighting, but I did not because I had seen what Taylor's men were doing in Kakata—stealing from the people and killing anyone who opposed them. I also knew Roosevelt Johnson would never allow himself to be arrested.

I told Reverend Kofi it was not safe to stay on Fifth Street anymore and we needed to get him and all of the orphans to Mamba Point, where the US embassy was. He said that it was a good idea, and we started transporting people in an ACFI van to the home of one of our church members, Mother Juah Buchanan, who lived close to the embassy. By Liberian standards, Mother Buchanan was wealthy. She owned two homes—a small house on Lynch Street and a two-story house with eight rooms on Mamba Point where she lived.

After my first trip to Mamba Point, I told Rebecca to take Joshua and go to my Uncle Galamue's place—the brother of the aunty we had brought from Yowee. He lived on Capital Bypass close to the University of Liberia's main campus.

Peters and I decided that the ACFI orphans and the blind men could stay on Fifth Street at the headquarters, because we had plenty of food and drinking water there. We felt because the children were orphans and the men were all blind, people would take pity on them and not harm them.

Also, the wife of Wilton Sankawolo, the chairman of the council of state, knew the orphan children were at ACFI because she had brought us our first and second group of orphans. So Peters and I thought she would surly ask her husband to tell Taylor to send men to guard the orphans and blind men.

We were so wrong.

By one thirty that Saturday afternoon, the fighting had spread all the way up to Ninth Street and was very close to the ACFI headquarters on Fifth Street. Peters stayed with the orphans and the blind men at the ACFI compound while I took my two brothers and seven or eight older men and women to Mother Buchanan's house in Mamba Point. When I got there, Peters called me on my cell phone and said the ACFI compound was too dangerous for the orphans, and he wanted me to come back and get the orphans while he led the blind men to Mother Buchanan's. Any car I used would have been taken from me at that point, so I ran back to Fifth Street with a young man from the church.

When we got to the ACFI headquarters, Peters told me some of Johnson's soldiers were running down the beach, trying to join up with Johnson and the rest of the ULIMO-J at the Barclay Training Center, and NPFL soldiers were chasing after them. We could not go that way.

It would have been too hard for Peters to take the blind men, so he decided to stay there with them and try to get out the next day. I took the orphans over to Lynch Street and then went back to the headquarters to get some sleeping clothes for them. When I made it back to them, they were all scared and hungry. Lynch Street was very close to the Barclay Training Center, where Johnson was holed up and the fighting was heavy, so I couldn't keep the children there. I decided to take them to Mother Buchanan's.

It was far too dangerous to move in a large group with the nearby fighting and bullets whizzing everywhere, so I divided the nine children into two groups. I took the first group to Mother Buchanan's smaller house on Lynch Street, where the fighting would be south of us. I went back for the second group, and we joined up with the first group. Then we all walked to Mother Buchanan's house on Mamba Point in a straight line. God miraculously brought us all safe through the danger to Mamba Point, and we were able to get something to eat.

At midnight, I received a call from Peters. Taylor's NPFL had taken over the ACFI headquarters and ordered all nine of them, Peters and the blind men, outside. They kicked them and fired their guns into the sand to make them leave. Then they brought in a truck to haul out any food or anything else of value on the grounds.

The next morning, Peters led the blind men southeast through Taylor's control area, thinking they might find some help, but it was not to be. Peters had to lead them all on foot from Fifth Street southeast to Red Light and all the way up and around to New Kru Town on Bushrod Island, north of Monrovia—much the same trip we had made the day before in Reverend Kofi's car.

The little food we had at Mother Buchanan's ran out, so we had to come up with a plan to get the orphans to New Kru Town. New Kru Town would be somewhat safer for them, because ECOMOG forces were nearby and some food could be found. Reverend Kofi asked Peters to find a way to Mamba Point so he could take the orphans back to New Kru town, to a woman named Ma Esther. Reverend Kofi had asked Ma Esther to take care of the children until the fighting was settled around the ACFI headquarters.

I remember the faces of those orphans: Kerkula, Jude, Galama, Motama, Josephine, Cecelia, and the rest.

While we were at Mother Buchanan's house on Mamba Point, Taylor's NPFL and Kromah's ULIMO-K were constantly troubling us. Every night, they carried out secret killings in the area. One day, a friend of mine, who was a government police officer, came and told me Taylor was sending men to kill Samuel Dokie. Dokie was one of the leaders of the CRC-NPFL, which split from Taylor's NPFL in September 1994. Dokie was living right next door to our refuge at Mother Buchanan's. It was late in the afternoon, and we could not immediately move out of the house with all the people we had with us. There were seventy-five to eighty people taking shelter in Mother Buchanan's house.

By this time the government was mostly controlled by Taylor, because he had the largest military force. My police friend told me he would be coming along with Taylor's men to arrest Dokie. So that night when Taylor's men came for Dokie, my friend came and called out to me in Mother Buchanan's so I would know he was there. He protected us that night and stopped the soldiers from coming into the house and stealing everything we had, beating us, and even killing us.

Every one of us in Mother Buchanan's house was afraid that night. Nobody even moved. But I heard my police friend outside talking to a group of Taylor's soldiers, so I decided to go out to the gate of the house. He had told me he would talk loud so I would know he was around. As I was about to leave the house, I heard people telling me not to, but I still went. I got to the gate and told my friend I was there. He told me to come outside so we could talk a little. I opened the gate and stepped out. My friend told me Taylor's soldiers had gone to the house next door to arrest Dokie, but he was not there, so instead they looted the house and tried to burn it down.

I asked him if it was still safe for us to stay, and he told me we should spend the night at Mother Buchanan's but leave in the morning. He said soldiers would keep coming around looking for Dokie. So I told Reverend Kofi it was not safe to stay at Mother Buchanan's any longer. I was afraid Taylor's men might find us and claim, because Dokie was not in the house next door, we had helped Dokie escape and were against Taylor and must know where Dokie was. Taylor's NPFL soldiers could never be trusted. They would lie about anyone just to get them into trouble or loot everything they had. Also, Reverend Kofi was well known, and people had the idea he was rich because Americans visited him and he also traveled to America. This put all of us at risk, because Taylor's soldiers, like other soldiers, would stop at nothing to find money or valuables.

Reverend Kofi agreed we should move from Mother Buchanan's and go to Greystone, which was about three blocks away. The Greystone compound was an IDP camp about one block from the US embassy and was owned and controlled by the embassy. It was a walled compound consisting of a large open field on a slight hill with a couple of buildings. Many civilians ended up taking refuge from the fighting there, hoping they would be safe.

We thought Greystone would be a safer place than any other IDP camp, and the morning after Taylor's men came for Dokie, we started asking our church members and relatives in Mother Buchanan's house to begin moving to Greystone.

After we made sure everyone had left the house, Reverend Kofi and I were alone with Mother Buchanan. And she absolutely refused to leave. Reverend Kofi was trying hard to convince her when, all of a sudden, fighting erupted nearby. It was heavy fighting, and bullets were whizzing about outside and smacking into the side of the house. I told Reverend Kofi to go while I helped Mother Buchanan. I put Mother Buchanan on my back and took off running. She was very heavy, and I was exhausted by the time we reached Greystone.

The US embassy had ordered the gate to Greystone locked because the fighting was now so close. We appealed to the security guards to please open them for us, but they were so afraid for their lives and their jobs they refused to let us in—they were private security hired by the embassy, and they were unarmed. Then one of the head security guards saw I had an old lady with me, so he told another guard to hurry and open the gate for us. Thank God for that man.

We could have been killed so easily that day, and many Liberian civilians did lose their lives trying to get to Greystone. Some of them died right outside the gate. I remember seeing so many dead Liberians that day I lost count as to how many. We were the last people they let into Greystone that afternoon. Thank God Mother Buchanan was with us.

We thought because the US embassy owned Greystone, we would be protected there. This was not the case. Taylor's NPFL controlled the area around Greystone, and because the Greystone guards were unarmed, soldiers came into the camp whenever they wanted. They arrested and killed anyone in the camp they thought was an enemy.

Still, Greystone was somewhat safer than other camps. Though, we were miserable. Many of us slept out in the open, because there was not enough space in the buildings for everyone. It was the rainy season in Liberia, and we had nowhere to go to get out of the torrential rains.

Greystone became unbearable. At first, we had only rain water to drink, though later the US embassy brought drinking water to us in a tanker truck. And we did everything inside the fence of the compound. One area of the compound was used for a toilet and a dump site, and when it rained, the runoff flowed right down the hill to where we slept, carrying human waste and garbage with it. Joshua was only about one and a half years old. I remember lying down on the ground at night to sleep and holding him on my stomach to protect him from the filthy water that would run down the hill and flow all around us. The place smelled awful, and many children and elderly people died from cholera, diarrhea, and malnourishment. People of all ages might die from a stray bullet.

After several weeks, I could not stand it any longer. I just wanted to die so I would not have to see my wife and small boy suffering. I asked God to take my life. I knew a person could be killed by a stray bullet, and I wanted this to happen to me, but it did not, so one day, I decided to go outside the compound fence to be killed directly by a soldier.

Civilians were only allowed outside the fence when there was no fighting going on in the area. There had been a lot of fighting around Greystone during the night, but I made up my mind to go out anyway. I kept my plans a secret. If I had told Rebecca about what I wanted to do, she would never have let me go. I didn't even tell her I was going toward the fence. None of my friends or relatives knew what I was going to do.

The gate to Greystone was usually opened early in the morning while the embassy security guards changed shifts. That day, I woke up early, and while the gate was open for the changing of the guards, I went out.

Once I was through the gate, I immediately saw three dead bodies lying outside the compound fence. Instantly, three of Taylor's NPFL charged up to me and demanded I bury the bodies, but I refused. By this time, everyone inside the fence saw what was going on. Some pleaded with me to just bury the bodies. They didn't want the soldiers to kill me, but that's what I wanted. When I refused to obey them, the soldiers started beating me with their guns, but right then an NPFL general arrived and asked the soldiers what they were doing. The soldiers told the general I would not carry out their orders.

This general's fighting name was General Satan. Many generals took a fighting name different than their own, and many of these names came from American movies or news reports, such as

General Rambo or General Bin Laden. To become a general, one had to be able to lead soldiers and to kill. One became a general by being a very wicked man.

As it turned out, General Satan knew me well. He had lived with me at the church building in the Buzzie Quarter during the early part of the war, when he was not fighting with the NPFL. He ordered the soldiers to stop beating me and told them I was his pappy. He told them never to make trouble for me again or he would kill them himself. He even ordered them to make sure I was safe from other NPFL soldiers. Then General Satan told me to go back inside the compound, so back I went.

Everyone told me I was lucky. Again, I was not lucky; I was protected and blessed by God almighty, in spite of my desire to be killed. Where is God in war? Right beside me, where He always is, even when I stray from the path. Even though the man who saved me called himself General Satan, he rescued a child of God. If he had not known me, I am sure the lawless men of Taylor's NPFL would have killed me then and there.

That day, I was saved by God again. But I was not happy about it. I had wanted to die. Rebecca and many others asked me why I did something so stupid. I responded that because of the terrible situation, I just wanted the soldiers to kill me. From that time on, my wife always watched me very carefully to see where I was and what I was doing.

My life is not more important than those many other Liberians who died. But God saved my life for reasons best known to Himself. God is good. He has a plan for everyone. Even though I decided to give up my own life, God protected me. And I know he saved many other lives during the Liberian Civil War.

Sometimes, the NPFL brought looted goods to the gate of the Greystone compound to sell to us. The soldiers brought food, clothing, and anything else they had stolen from people's homes. Sometimes we would buy our own belongings from them. Sometimes we would see our own clothes on the soldiers, but we dared not ask for the items back, or we might have been killed.

There was no law in the land. Those who carried guns were the authorities. They did whatever they wanted, and no one could stop them. Soldiers could kill anyone at any time for whatever reason they wanted. They could take anything someone had if they wanted it. Sometimes a civilian would be forced to take off his shoes or shirt or trousers, or anything else a soldier wanted, and there was nothing anybody could do about it.

During Charles Taylor's attempt to arrest Roosevelt Johnson, many appeals went out to Taylor at his house in Congo Town to ask his men to stop the fighting, but Taylor did not heed these pleas. The Interfaith Mediation Committee asked him to stop the fighting, but still he refused.

Soldiers from the NPFL were still coming into Greystone whenever they wanted to arrest and kill anyone they thought might be against Taylor. But this came to a stop when all of us inside the compound agreed we would not allow any more of us to be arrested and taken away, even if that person was a former fighter. We all said if a fighter laid down his gun and ran inside the fence for refuge, he would be protected. A group of us went to the US embassy and requested they support this decision, and they agreed to stop allowing Taylor's men to come into Greystone. Taylor's forces were informed if they entered the compound, the US marines assigned to the embassy would respond with force. This was a blessing, and many lives were saved.

As for Roosevelt Johnson, he and his ULIMO-J were still holding the Barclay Training Center and the surrounding area. They were not fighting to gain ground but to defend their territory and their lives. However, though Taylor had more troops and arms, he still could not defeat Johnson's soldiers.

One of Johnson's generals rose to prominence during the April fighting in Monrovia. His name was Joshua Blahyi, but he called himself General Butt Naked. Blahyi claims he was initiated as a tribal priest and participated in his first human sacrifice at age eleven. During the course of the three-day ritual, Blahyi says he had a vision in which he was told by the Devil he would become a great warrior and he should continue to practice human sacrifice and cannibalism to increase his power. Krahn elders later appointed him as a high priest, a position that would lead him to become the spiritual advisor to Samuel Doe after he assumed the presidency. After Doe was killed, Blahyi became a general and took the name General Butt Naked. He and his soldiers—men, women, and many children—all went into battle naked. April 6, 1996, was the first-time Liberians saw naked fighters in the streets of Monrovia.

General Butt Naked was a very strong fighter. Many times, Taylor's NPFL ran away from Butt Naked's soldiers. Whenever

NPFL soldiers heard, "Move it!" they fled for their lives. This was a war cry Krahn and Butt Naked's soldiers used.

Taylor's NPFL tried many times to take Johnson's stronghold at the Barclay Training Center, but Johnson's few troops, including those who fought for General Butt Naked, always fought them back. Taylor's soldiers would sometimes even try to run into Greystone to escape.

By the grace of God, the international community was eventually able to convince Taylor to stop the fighting. I am certain the United States was part of this process.

The resolution to end the fighting came through the United Nations in 1996. The UN asked Taylor and Johnson's ULIMO-J to put down their arms and give the suffering people of Monrovia a chance to return to their homes. Johnson was never arrested by Taylor, but thousands of men, women, and children lost their lives. Many homes and other buildings were burned down by both sides. There was no winner in this battle, but the people of Monrovia were the losers.

I personally cannot find any reason why Taylor started the fighting in Monrovia on April 6. Perhaps Taylor simply wanted to show Roosevelt Johnson he was more powerful than any other Liberian warlord. Many Liberians, including myself, want to know the real reason. Taylor's attempt to arrest Johnson and continued refusal to give it up made many Liberians believe Taylor did not truly love the nation and people of Liberia the way he said he did and only wanted power and control.

We lived in Greystone almost four months, from April to the end of July. I was part of the first group of people who left the compound after the fighting subsided. I took with me some of the young men of our church who were also living in Greystone. We went to check on our homes and the ACFI headquarters. We found at the headquarters that only the buildings were left. Everything else had been looted. We knew Taylor's NPFL had done this, even though they called themselves government forces and were supposed to be protecting our lives and property. They took everything from our poor homes, even the doors, bathroom fixtures, electrical wiring from inside the walls, and floor mats.

We started cleaning right away, but we had to be back inside Greystone by six in the evening. Civilians were not allowed to be on the street after six. We took a few days going back and forth to clean up the headquarters. Eventually, some of the young men of the church and some of the pastors, including myself, spent several nights there before we brought the women and children home.

After my family returned to the Sinkor District, we slept in a house that had no doors, and we slept on the cement floor. We had to start life all over again. God protected us during all this time. Life had to go on, in spite of the shortage of food or other necessities. Our church headquarters was right on the ocean, and the young men living there with us were able to hunt for crabs every night on the beach. We would boil the crabs in water with collard greens and make a soup for our one meal each day. It was not the first time I had lost all my belongings, but I grieved for my family.

Eventually, the international community was able to send aid through nongovernmental organizations. Thank God for the compassion of those in other countries who gave help to the Liberian people at this time.

After we moved back home, I found myself doing what I love to do best: helping people. I helped people clean their homes, comforted people with the Word of God, and encouraged people to put the past behind them and strive to move forward. I feel called to help people to move forward in life. We cannot continue to look at our past. We need to forget the past and move forward.

Working particularly with orphans and widows at this time was a balm to my heart. We at ACFI started particularly helping orphans and widows, and I was involved in working with the many children who had lost their parents during the fighting. Many of these children witnessed the deaths of their parents. We were able to set up an orphanage for some of them, and we also helped orphans who lived in other orphanages.

One of the causes I became most interested in was discouraging children from being soldiers. There were many children involved in the fighting in Liberia who were used by the warlords to carry guns and kill. Our future leaders were being recruited by Taylor's NPFL first and then by other factions. I felt heartbroken every time I saw a child carrying a gun.

It was often apparent these children had been drugged by their warlords with any number of substances: alcohol, marijuana, hashish, opium, gun powder mixed into milk, or cocaine rubbed into cuts on their faces or arms. Child soldiers were given pills, probably amphetamines, which were sometimes called *bubbles* because of the high they gave. All this was done so the children would have no feelings when killing.

The desire to educate these children grew strong on my mind. Education, I knew, was going to be key in restoring these children. The Bible says people perish because of a lack of knowledge. This is what was going on with these children. They lacked education. The Devil loves for people to have no knowledge of the truth:

So Christ himself gave the apostles, the prophets, the evangelists, the pastors and teachers, to equip his people for works of service, so that the body of Christ may be built up until we all reach unity in the faith and in the knowledge of the Son of God and become mature, attaining to the whole measure of the fullness of Christ. Then we will no longer be infants, tossed back and forth by the waves, and blown here and there by every wind of teaching and by the cunning and craftiness of people in their deceitful scheming. Instead, speaking the truth in love, we will grow to become in every respect the mature body of him who is the head, that is, Christ. (Ephesians 4:11-15)

Carrying guns and killing had become normal for these children. Carrying a gun also became for them a symbol of power and authority. Fathers and mothers were forced to submit to their children because their children carried guns.

I concluded these children needed education instead of guns. This was the beginning of my desire to pray and ask God to provide the means. It had been almost eight years of war since many of these children had been able to have access to education.

I was able to use some of my time after Greystone to talk to children and child soldiers about the dangers of carrying guns.

In September 1996, Ruth Perry became chairwoman of the Council of State of Liberia. Madam Perry was the fourth interim government leader since Doe's death, and she led Liberia to an elected government in July 1997.

The election in 1997 was the election that finally brought Charles Taylor to power as president of Liberia.

11 ~ ALL GOD'S CHILDREN

It was after the April 1996 fighting in Monrovia that I became involved in starting the All God's Children (AGC) school system. The idea began with my meeting two men from the United States the previous year.

Steve Jones had been a member of a mission team from Fellowship Bible Church in Tacoma, Washington, in 1995. The mission team came to Liberia to conduct leadership training and revival meetings through ACFI. Fellowship Bible Church was also involved in sending financial aid and humanitarian supplies to Liberia. Steve and I became friends, and he told me his younger brother, Nathan, would be coming to Liberia to do some photography work for World Vision. Steve wanted me to help his brother while he was in Liberia, and when Steve went back to the US, he told Nathan about me.

Figure 1. Child Soldier with AK-47 rifle

On Nathan Jones's first trip to Liberia in 1995, he asked me to go along with him to take photos of child soldiers. Nathan and I visited various IDP camps inside and outside of Monrovia, taking photos for World Vision. He took the photos, and I acted as a guide and helped carry his equipment.

During this trip, I remember Nathan asked me the question, "What do you advise if someone wants to help in the Liberia situation?"

My answer to him was education.

Nathan's second question was, "Why education?"

My answer was because education cannot be taken away from a

child, or an adult.

Every other kind of relief, such as clothes or money, could be taken away from anyone during this period of war. The Liberian people needed to be educated, especially the children. They needed to know that guns and killing were not the answer to the situation. The children needed an education to give them hope and a future beyond killing.

Nathan returned to the US, and on his second trip to Liberia in 1996, again for World Vision, he brought many disposable cameras with him. Nathan and I took these cameras and gave them to child soldiers. He asked them to take any photos they liked. The children took photos and returned the cameras to us.

Also on this trip, Nathan asked me the same questions he had asked before, about how to help in Liberia. I gave him the same answers. At this time, he told me nothing about his intention of opening a school in Liberia for children impacted by the war.

On this second trip, Nathan had to flee Liberia after the fighting began in April.

While Nathan was home in the US, he met with his brother Steve and Doug Collier, who also attended Fellowship Bible Church in Tacoma, and he told them stories about the estimated thirty to forty thousand war orphans in Liberia's capital city of Monrovia. These orphans had no opportunity to return to school because the educational system in Liberia had been completely destroyed. They had no parents and no way to take care of themselves. The only option for survival left to these children was to return to fighting.

Moved by the troubles of the many children whose lives had been devastated by the war, Nathan, Steve, and Doug decided to create a 501(c)(3) non-profit organization based in Tacoma and called it All God's Children. Doug is a CPA and knew how to file all of the necessary paperwork. They raised money to finance a free school for war orphans, ex-combatants, and other children who were too poor to pay for school.

In February 1997, Nathan called me and asked me to be involved in starting this school for orphans and child soldiers. Of course, I agreed.

Nathan and Steve Jones and Doug Collier put together support for our first free-education school in the Sinkor District of Monrovia. The founding mission of All God's Children was to take guns from the hands of children and give them an education.

This was a huge blessing and answer to prayer. This had been my heart's cry.

We focused on child soldiers and other children who were at risk for being recruited to fight. The plan was to have morning and afternoon sessions, with fifty different children in each. But because of the difficult situation in Liberia at the time, with so much fighting still going on in the rural areas, I decided to do only one session in the morning for all of the students. Parents and guardians did not want their children to be away from home in the afternoon, when it was more dangerous to be out.

During this time, there were regular attempts to broker a cease-fire between the major warring factions, but all held to their control areas and continued to fight. The major factions included: Charles Taylor's NPFL, which still controlled most of Liberia; Alhaji Kromah's ULIMO-K, which controlled, in large part, the border with Sierra Leone; Roosevelt Johnson's ULIMO-J, which held on to parts of Monrovia; George Boley's Liberia Peace Council, which controlled a portion of Liberia in the southwest; and a group called the Lofa Defense Force, which formed in 1993 and was headed by Francois Massaquoi, who later became minister of sport, and controlled most of Lofa County.

The United States was working with the international community to find lasting peace in Liberia, and the United Nations was involved with relief efforts and much needed humanitarian aid.

Part of my work became to identify child soldiers and work with them to leave their guns and killing and turn to education, which would give them a future. I already knew a lot of these children, and they remembered when Nathan and I had given them cameras to take photos, so they knew me too. I was their contact between Nathan and AGC. Some children took advantage of our offer and enrolled in our school, while others refused to lay down their guns.

There was danger in what I was attempting to do, because I was taking child soldiers away from warlords. But I did not care then about what some warlord might have done to me. I only wanted as many children away from killing and in school as possible.

I also went from home to home where displaced children were staying to recruit for our school. Some of these were children living on their own, living with extended families, or living in orphanages.

Nathan asked me to recruit 100 students, but it only took two weeks for me to find 150 children who wanted to enroll. It was very difficult for me to turn down children who wanted to learn, and I ended up with over 180 students.

The new AGC school was a lot of work. I had to put together the best teaching staff I could. This was tough, because almost everyone with an education had left the country, leaving few qualified teachers to choose from. In addition, everyone still in the country needed a job. People were desperate, and they looked to me for the hope of a job to provide for their families, even if they did not meet my high standard of having a teaching certificate. How do you tell someone they are not going to be hired when you know their family is starving?

There were many struggles involved in setting up this first AGC school. Many people did not believe it was going to work. Some of my friends were afraid for me because of the warlords, but God was in control. This opportunity was important for so many children, and it was worth the risks.

We opened the first All God's Children school in January 1997 in a rented warehouse. The United States Agency for International Development had used the warehouse before the war to store supplies but had abandoned it during the fighting, as happened with so many other businesses and international aid organizations. We used braided bamboo to divide the seven-hundred-square-foot space into three classrooms for the ABC class (nursery school), the K-1 (pre-school) and K-2 (kindergarten) classes, and the first-grade class.

Doug Collier was my boss. I reported to him. He helped raise funds to operate the schools with Steve and Nathan, and he would send me the money via Western Union. I would send Doug monthly reports that accounted for the funds we spent on salaries, supplies, etc. Eventually, our employer-employee relationship developed into a brotherly relationship that will continue for the rest of our lives.

Doug made his first two-week trip to Liberia in April 1997, during our first school year. The reality of the difficult situation in Liberia was all too apparent to Doug as we drove from Roberts International Airport to Monrovia. The streets of every town were full of combatants, many of whom were young children carrying AK-47 rifles.

Doug and I attended meetings almost every day with relief organizations, such as World Vision, and met with officials from the United Nations involved in education projects. Because Doug is a white man, he was able to go to meetings that were normally closed to me as a black Liberian. The organizations did not trust Liberians. For example, we once called on the World Vision office located on Mamba Point in Monrovia. World Vision was one of the many organizations working with the UN to provide aid to the Liberian people. I went to the gate and asked if we could come in. The security guard told me no, but when he saw Doug, he immediately opened the gate and allowed us in.

Doug and I also visited several possible sites for future schools. One was deep in the jungle in a small village called Zordi. Passing through other villages on the way to Zordi was heartbreaking. We saw the terrible impact the war had on remote villages. The mud huts had bullet holes in them, and young people were mostly nowhere to be seen—they had been killed or captured or had fled into the jungle when soldiers from various factions came through the area, looting, raping, and killing. We had to make the very tough decision to not open a school in Zordi due to its remote location, which made travel to Zordi difficult and dangerous.

In the following year, the enrollment of AGC grew from 180 to over 1,200 students, and our staff grew to forty-five. We grew from an ABC through first grade school to a full elementary school— ABC through sixth grade.

This was also a major time of transition for Liberia, which though technically democratic for 150 years, for the first time moved toward a multi-party democratic republic. Presidential and congressional elections were scheduled in Liberia for May 1997, but all elections were postponed by the UN until July 1997 to allow more time for voter registration, because of the many logistical challenges to registration due to most of Liberia's infrastructure being lost in the war. The election commission also faced challenges in educating the public about voting and the discretion involved in voting. An estimated 70 to 90 percent of the population were illiterate, making it even more difficult to educate them.

The three faction leaders of the council of state, Charles Taylor, Alhaji Kromah, and George Boley, resigned from their positions so they could run for president. There were sixteen parties who participated in the elections altogether, with Taylor from the National Patriotic Party and Ellen Johnson Sirleaf from the Unity Party leading the presidential race. There was a large voter turnout of 89 percent, and there was 1 election observer per 280 voters. The elections were overseen by 469 foreign observers from the United Nations, the Economic Community of West African States, and the Carter Center (former US president Jimmy Carter and his wife both observed the election). In addition, there were 1,800 locally trained election observers.

At the time, many Liberians felt bringing Taylor to power through a democratic election would mean peace for Liberia. They were afraid if Taylor did not become president, the war would not come to an end. Taylor himself would publicly reference the Liberian proverb, *No monkey work, baboon draws*. This meant, if Taylor did the work, someone else should not take the credit. Taylor believed he had done the hard work and was not willing to see some so-called Liberian politician enjoy the power and recognition he had fought for for all those years.

During the election campaign, some of Taylor's supporters came up with the slogan, "You killed my ma, you killed my pa, I will vote for you." Many Liberians went to the street chanting this slogan. This was an attempt to intimidate Liberians into voting for Taylor, suggesting if they did not vote for him, Taylor would continue to fight and the civil war would start all over again, and to many war-weary Liberians, this was a very real concern.

Liberians wanted peace. If this meant electing a killer, so be it.

Figure 2. Charles Taylor Casting his vote

On July 19, 1997, more than 750,000 Liberians cast their votes, and Charles Taylor won with 75 percent of the vote. Ellen Johnson Sirleaf came in at a distant second with 9 percent, and Alhaji Kromah was third with 4 percent of the vote.

I voted for Ellen Johnson Sirleaf, because I believed she was not involved in any of the fighting. Later, I learned Sirleaf was actually one of the founders of the National Patriotic Front of Liberia, Taylor's faction, and was a powerful part of the organization. However, after she saw Taylor was not willing to step down from power and let anyone else in, she left the NPFL and formed her own political party.

So after seven years of civil war, Taylor was finally given what he could not take militarily—the presidency of Liberia.

Charles Taylor was inaugurated on August 2, 1997.

Everyone hoped the election of Charles Taylor meant Liberia would be a peaceful nation once again, and it was for almost three years. During these three years, many Liberians tried to find lost family members among the various IDP camps in Liberia and refugee camps in surrounding countries. Many families were split up when soldiers had invaded their village or town and they had fled in different directions. It took some families years to determine what had happened to their dispersed family members. Some families will never know what happened to their loved ones.

There was still no electricity or running water in Monrovia, a city of over one million people. Government schools were not open, there was no garbage collection, and there were very few bathrooms. No ambulance service existed, and only a few medical professionals remained in the entire country. Most of us were completely dependent on the United Nations for clean water and food. But because we had peace, Liberians began to rebuild and start our lives over again.

Rebecca and I decided to move to a house in Matadi, just south of the Sinkor District. The house was a cement block structure, like most houses in Liberia, and was about nine hundred square feet of living quarters. We had no running water or electricity at the house.

In 1999, three additional AGC schools were opened in rural areas of Liberia, thanks to a $100,000 grant we received from Adventist Relief Agency (ADRA) out of Sweden. We built one school on the Firestone Rubber Tree Plantation that we called the Civil Compound. We also remodeled a Firestone building located at 15 Gate on the Firestone Rubber Tree Plantation into a school—we called this school 15 Gate. And finally, we rented a building for a school in a town located in Lofa County near the border of Guinea called Voingama.

The ADRA grant provided uniforms, chairs, and all the

materials needed to operate the schools for one year, but after that time, AGC would have to fund all of these things ourselves.

Almost four thousand children who had no other access to education were served by AGC during these three years of peace, receiving education, counseling, and food.

Our goals at AGC have not only included educating these children, but also helping them move forward in life after the horrors of the war. Since the beginning of AGC, our one full-time Christian counselor, David Golowa, has helped former child soldiers and non-combatants to deal with the traumas they experienced during the war and the deprivation of post-war living and to work toward healing and restoration in their lives. I was also part of the counseling process during this time.

Many Liberian children witnessed atrocities against their families and friends during the war, and some were combatants who committed atrocities themselves. In addition to the traumas of war, the child soldiers we worked with needed to confront all the things they had done, and we developed a three-step process to help child soldiers reintegrate into society.

The first step was building trust between our staff and the child soldiers. Many of these young children had experienced all kinds of violence in their lives, and they needed a safe place to talk these things through without fear of being judged for what they themselves might have done.

The second step involved creating a loving environment. These children went from being innocent children to vicious killers without remorse. They needed to experience a loving relationship. Many child soldiers were shunned after the war for the things they did. We wanted to love these children.

The final step was meeting the needs of former child soldiers according to God's Word. We wanted to show these children that we loved them and that Christ loved them, regardless of what they had done. We wanted to replace the hopelessness they faced with the forgiveness, peace, and purpose of life that only Christ can give.

The war started again in 1999. Our schools continued to operate until they were forced to close due to fighting and looting. In July 2000, the school in Voingama was completely destroyed by a new rebel faction called Liberians United for Reconciliation and Democracy (LURD).

Figure 3. Father and child fleeing the fighting

LURD was made up of Mandingo and Krahn tribesmen and operated from Guinea. A few of our staff members from the Voingama school were able to flee to Monrovia, including one of the teachers, James Akoi, and the principal, Sarah Borzie, but most of the staff was killed or captured. Of the children, we only heard they fled into the jungle.

Rebecca and I wanted to wait until the war ended and things settled down before we had our next child, but we surprised ourselves again. Our second child was born on October 19, 2001, at Eternal Love Winning Africa Hospital (ELWA), a private, Christian hospital. Even though we lived very close to the John F. Kennedy Medical Center, where Joshua was born, Rebecca did not want to deliver our second child there. Because ELWA was a private hospital, it was more expensive than JFK but less crowded.

John F. Kennedy Medical Center was the only functioning government hospital operating in Liberia at this time, and it was completely overcrowded with sick and dying patients. There were too few doctors and nurses with too little medicine to care for all of the patients, and many died every day. If a family member did not claim a body, the hospital staff buried the dead on the hospital grounds or on the beach facing the hospital. There were many amputations at the hospital, and the stench from the decaying arms and legs was horrible. I went by JFK almost every day on my way to our AGC school in Monrovia to look for friends or family who might have been wounded. Every time I went, there were more dead bodies.

Rebecca was sick a lot during her second pregnancy. She had to go to ELWA many times, and this was a major struggle. We had to get up very early and arrive at the hospital first thing in the morning if we wanted a chance to meet with a doctor or nurse.

Even though ELWA was not as busy as JFK, due to the war, there was never enough staff available to handle all of the patients in a timely fashion. Sometimes when Rebecca felt sick, I had to go to work or look for food, so she would have to make the long trip alone or with her close friend, Rhoda. But even though she often felt sick, she was still excited for our second child to come. Rebecca was sure she was having a girl this time and had chosen a name, Patience. She had even purchased some girl baby clothes.

As before, the war was terrible. Many people were dying from the fighting, hunger, and disease. There was a common saying in Liberia during this time, "Death is better than life." There was no electricity, no running water or safe water to drink, and food was almost impossible to buy. I sometimes wondered how we were going to survive with another child. I believe it is only because of God my family and others were able to survive.

Usually, Liberians eat rice every day. But during this time, rice, again, was very expensive and almost impossible to find. The only supply of rice was at Freeport, which was now controlled by LURD. The area where we lived, in Matadi, was controlled by Taylor and the government, and we were separated from Freeport by the Mesurado River. We had to depend on the few international organizations still operating in Liberia. They provided us with bulgur wheat in place of rice.

We had a lot of friends and family living at our house in Matadi, and finding enough food was hard. We ate whatever we could. We ate grass or plants, and many times, we went days without food. We drank a lot of pepper soup, and sometimes we had fish to put in it—I made friends with some local river fishermen and told them to please remember my family whenever they had fish or crab to sell, especially because my wife was pregnant. The hot, spicy soup made our stomachs feel full.

Clean drinking water was also very hard to find, but we could get drinking water from the well on the AGC school campus in the Sinkor District. There was also a well in Matadi, but we only used the water from the Matadi well for bathing and cooking, if we had something to cook.

One day toward the end of her pregnancy, Rebecca was experiencing a lot of pain, so we took her to ELWA. They examined her and said the baby was not ready to be delivered yet, so we went home. Rebecca was in terrible pain all day and night.

The next day I had to go look for food, and while I was gone, Rebecca and Rhoda decided to go back to ELWA.

After waiting several hours to see a nurse, they admitted Rebecca for observation. Rhoda returned to our house and told me Rebecca was spending the night at the hospital and she needed food and clothes. The hospital was not able to provide these things, so it was up to family members to provide them. Rhoda returned to the hospital while I went to find what Rebecca needed, and after Rhoda arrived back at the hospital, Rebecca gave birth to our baby. Rhoda ran back to our house to find me and tell me the good news.

I returned home from shopping for Rebecca, and while I was praying for her, Rhoda came running in. She asked me to guess if the baby was a boy or a girl. I told her it was a girl, but she said it was a boy. I thought she was joking, because Rebecca had been positive she was having a girl. Rhoda tried to convince me, but I still thought it was a joke. She asked for some money to buy a bathtub for our newest child, so I gave her the money. In Liberian culture, it is traditional, if the baby is a girl, to buy a pink bathtub and, if the baby is a boy, to buy a blue one. Of course, I was expecting Rhoda to bring back a pink tub, but she returned with a blue tub, and I finally believed her that I had another son.

I returned to the hospital with Rhoda to meet our new son and to choose a name for him. Names are important. I chose to name our new son Caleb Sackie Kwalalon. In Numbers 13, Joshua and Caleb went to spy out the promised land and returned with good news for the children of Israel. Our two sons were our good news to us during those trying times.

Caleb has grown up strong, and I praise God for bringing me and my family such a long way.

Before Rebecca became pregnant with Caleb, she had planned to go to the United States to study nursing. We worked with Doug Collier and his sister Barbara and were able to complete the visa application and Rebecca was accepted to Tacoma Community College in Washington. We had decided to send Joshua with her to the US. He was big for only being seven years old, and we were concerned a faction might try to force him to join them. It would also be safer for him because I was often a target of soldiers because of my association with Americans. Anyone who had regular dealings with Americans was thought to have money, and even if this was not true, I stood a chance of being killed.

When Rebecca became pregnant with Caleb, we put off Rebecca's schooling. We waited until Caleb was eleven months old and started the application process for her student visa to the US again. But because her original application only had Rebecca and Joshua's names on it, the US embassy would not let Caleb be included on a new visa application. This forced us to make a hard decision: should Rebecca and Joshua go to the US and leave Caleb in Liberia with me?

Rebecca did not want to leave Caleb behind because he was so young. And I, as a typical Liberian man, had very little knowledge about how to care for a baby. Babies seem to cry for no reason, and they need their diapers changed often; these were all things I had no experience handling. I asked my sister, who was living with us at the time, if she would please help me with Caleb. She agreed.

Rebecca cried a lot about leaving Caleb, and she could not bring herself to make a decision. My main reason for wanting to send Rebecca and Joshua to the US was the war—I felt losing half of my family temporarily was better than losing all of us. When I told Rebecca my decision, she cried so much I almost changed my mind.

Rebecca decided we should meet with Pastor Dennis Gaye and ask for his advice. We both loved Pastor Gaye and respected his opinions. Pastor Gaye advised Rebecca to go to the US with Joshua. Rebecca's older sister, Mary, and my sister, Marion, also encouraged her to go.

Rebecca finally decided to go to the US with Joshua.

We reapplied for a US visa, and it was approved. Getting a US visa in Liberia is like winning the lottery. It is not an easy process, and few applications get approved. During the war, if you did get approved for a US visa, you had to keep it very quiet and only tell your closest friends. People would kill you for your visa and use it to leave the country. Procuring counterfeited documents to match the names already on a visa was very easy in a country where no functioning government existed to prevent this activity.

Rebecca and Joshua left for the US in August 2002. It was extremely emotional for me saying goodbye at the airport. Rebecca was weeping, and this caused me a lot of doubt. Was I doing the right thing? And some people might ask how a mother could leave her eleven-month-old child to be taken care of by others.

But we had prayed mightily and asked our friends for advice, and we took our time to make what we thought was the best decision for our family.

Monrovia, Liberia, to SeaTac, Washington, is 6,882 miles on a direct flight. But to get to SeaTac, it is typical to fly through Brussels and then to the United States. Rebecca and Joshua had never been more than 40 miles from their places of birth, or even on a plane, and now they were flying almost half way around the world by themselves. This fact added to my anxiety. But their flight went well, and Doug picked them up at the airport. As he was talking to them about their trip, he stepped on an escalator to go to baggage claim and continued talking. Halfway down the escalator he turned around and noticed that he was alone; Rebecca and Joshua were still at the top of the escalator. They had never seen an escalator before and did not know how to use it. Doug turned and ran back up the escalator to them. I wish I had a video of that.

Then when they arrived at Doug's house in Tacoma, Joshua looked out the window and saw a crow on the lawn. He said, "I will go and kill that bird and eat it." This was going to be a big adjustment for a young person who had never experienced electricity, running water, flushing toilets (actually, any toilet), television, frequently driving in a car, grocery shopping, and everything else many Americans take for granted.

Back in Liberia, taking care of Caleb helped me learn some lessons that often only mothers go through. Most African men leave all child care to the mother. But very quickly, I learned how to change Caleb's diaper, give Caleb a bath, and how to properly hold him. This was work I never saw myself doing. Taking care of Caleb was one of the most difficult jobs I have ever had, and I learned new gratitude for all mothers who do these things and more for their babies, and I learned patience.

In May 2002, LURD had captured Gbarnga, which had been Taylor's stronghold during the 1989–1999 fighting. LURD was now closing in on Monrovia. Fighting over Gbarnga continued for several months. Then in early 2003, a new faction who called themselves the Movement for Democracy in Liberia (MODEL) was formed by mostly Krahn tribesmen. MODEL invaded Liberia from the Ivory Coast and quickly allied themselves with LURD, because both groups fought for the common goal of removing Charles Taylor from the presidency.

All God's Children was forced to close the rural Civil Compound school in early 2003. It was too difficult to keep the school supplied because of the fighting in the area. When the conflict neared Monrovia in June of 2003, the remaining two AGC schools, 15 Gate and the Sinkor District school in Monrovia, were also forced to close. War had returned to Monrovia, and our staff and students had to run and find safety wherever they could.

The year 2003 was a very bad year. Pastor Gaye, the man who led me to the Lord, was hit by a stray bullet while he was searching for food and drinking water for his family. Pastor Gaye and his family had left their home on Camp Johnson Road and had gone to live in a deserted Mamba Point hotel. The hotel management had fled the country due to the war, and many people took refuge from the fighting in the deserted building, even though it was not an official IDP camp. The one caretaker left in charge of the hotel had been led to the Lord by Pastor Gaye, like myself, so he asked the pastor and his family to come stay at the hotel until it was safe for them to return home.

When I was told Pastor Gaye had been hit by a bullet, I immediately went to Mamba Point to find him. But by the time I reached the hotel, I was told by his wife he had been taken to JFK Medical Center. I made my way back to JFK as quickly as I could. When I finally saw my wounded pastor, I could not stand it and started to cry. He called me son and told me not to cry but to praise God I was able to find him in time.

The bullet was in Pastor Gaye's spinal cord, and there was no doctor able to operate and take it out. My friend and I decided to go in search of a native doctor, a man trained in traditional Liberian medicine, who we were told could remove the bullet. This man had probably learned how to remove bullets by helping wounded soldiers, though he had received no formal medical training in a modern school. This doctor was living across the St. Paul Bridge in an area now controlled by LURD. Another friend of mine, Al-Banto Momo, got into contact with the native doctor to ask if he could come help us, but the doctor could not cross the bridge. We could not go to him either because of the heavy fighting. We just had to wait and pray for the fighting to stop. In the meantime, I went to visit Pastor Gaye almost every time there was a way for me to do so.

Then we were told there was going to be a cease-fire between the factions. The night before the cease-fire, we were able to return Pastor Gaye to the hotel on Mamba Point where his family was still staying. The doctors at JFK had told us they could do nothing for him and told us to take him home. We contacted the native doctor again and told him someone would escort him to the hotel the next day while the cease-fire was in effect.

Early the next morning, I got up from bed and was on my way to see Pastor Gaye when I got a call on my cell phone. Pastor Gaye had died during the night. I ran all the way to Mamba Point and found that it was true. I quickly called the native doctor to tell him not to come because Pastor Gaye was already dead. We were then asked by Pastor Gaye's wife and our church leaders to bury Pastor Gaye at once, because we could not rely on the cease-fire to last. Normally, the body would be taken to a funeral home and prepared for burial. The funeral home would then take the body to an all-night wake at the family's home or church on a Friday night, and the body would be buried on a Saturday. I ran to my friend who was a casket maker and asked him to hurry and make a casket for my pastor's burial. My friend had one casket already made and sold it to me. We took the casket and were able to immediately bury Pastor Gaye.

Pastor Dennis Gaye was more than a pastor and friend to me. He led me to Christ and was very much involved in mentoring me in my Christian journey. I looked to him not only as a man of God but as a father. Remember, my parents were not around when I was a young man, so I did not always have fatherly love growing up. This man gave me that fatherly love. As a young pastor, I looked to him for advice in life and how to be a man of God. His death was so painful because of who he was to me and all he did for me while he was alive. His advice and good example continue to help me to be the man I am today.

I am glad I knew the Lord when Pastor Gaye died, or else I might have gone back to my old way of life because of what happened to him. I sometimes wonder why good people die. Why would God allow His servant to die like that when, as the Bible says, He is able to protect His people? I believe God wanted His servant to come home to rest from his labor. God is good all the time, and all the time He is good. We as humans might not understand how and why God works, but He is God, and we cannot question Him but only praise Him in season and out of season, for He is good.

Around this time, a group of Liberian women decided they needed to do something to help end the war, so they started meeting every day to pray and fast for Liberia and for peace. They were called the Women in White, because they always dressed in white t-shirts and blue *lapa* skirts. They met in the fish market of the Sinkor District in Monrovia. This place was right on the main road between the home of President Charles Taylor and the capital building, so he passed this place almost every day in his car.

These brave women held signs that Taylor could easily read as he drove to work each day. These signs read "Women Crying For Peace," "Our Nation Needs Peace," and "We Want Peace Now." The leaders of the Women in White even came together and asked Taylor to leave Liberia for the sake of peace. They stood strong in all weather—in rain or sunshine—and no threats could scare them away from meeting every day. They were a force for peace.

By May 2003, the LURD and MODEL factions controlled about 60 percent of Liberia, and Taylor was under intense pressure to step down as President. Peace talks started in Ghana in June between Taylor and the rebel factions. Many Liberian refugees who had fled to Ghana turned out to show support for peace during these talks. We Liberians, no matter where we lived, were incredibly frustrated by the lack of progress toward peace in Liberia and the political delays and blame games.

In June 2003, a new complication to the peace process arose: President Charles Taylor was publicly indicted for crimes against humanity by the Special Court for Sierra Leone (set up by Sierra Leone and the United Nations) while he was at the peace talks in Ghana. He had fomented the devastating war in Sierra Leone in the early 1990s and backed the rebel Revolutionary United Front, which had forced children to fight and had committed horrible atrocities during the war. This indictment of their enemy encouraged LURD and MODEL to continue the fighting.

The indictment also brought great fear in Monrovia that Taylor might be arrested while he was at the peace talks in Ghana. It might seem Monrovians would have wanted Taylor arrested, but this was not the case. You see, Taylor had left a trusted general, Benjamin Yeaten, in charge of his army while he was in Ghana. General Yeaten often threatened to go from house to house and kill anyone he thought was against Taylor. And if anyone arrested

Taylor while he was in Ghana, Yeaten said he and his soldiers would start shooting civilians on sight and turn Monrovia upside down. This man had a reputation of being very wicked in the eyes of many Liberians, including some of his own men, and we believed Yeaten truly would kill us all and destroy Liberia rather than see Taylor lose power.

In the end, the peace talks in Ghana came to nothing, and Taylor flew back to Liberia without being arrested. Monrovia was in darkness and nearly silent the night Taylor returned. Everybody looked for a place to hide themselves.

The fighting went on. The rebels were getting closer and closer to Monrovia. LURD launched rockets into the city and killed innocent civilians by the hundreds. Many Liberians fled to Greystone again to escape the fighting and shelling. As a nation, we pleaded with the US to send in troops as they had done for other countries and save the nation that was their step-child. The people seeking refuge at Greystone and others living around the US embassy started piling all the bodies of those killed by the rocket attacks from LURD or stray bullets or other causes in front of the embassy.

Doug Collier was in Liberia that June. He witnessed truckloads of dead combatants, many of them children, being taken away from the front lines. Sara, who traveled with Doug to Liberia, Jodi, a missionary from Oregon working with ACFI, Daniel, a World Vision employee from Kenya, and Doug were staying in a three-story building located on Sixth Street, the main road leading from the Sinkor District to downtown Monrovia. The building housed one whole floor of child soldiers recovering from wounds from the fighting. From that building, they could clearly hear AK-47s being fired and mortars exploding from all directions.

The fighting grew worse, and Doug, Sara, and Jodi were contacted by the US embassy and told all US personnel were being evacuated. MODEL had closed the road to the airport, so somehow, we had to make it to the embassy to get the Americans out of Liberia. Daniel had a World Vision van hidden inside the building's compound, and we decided to take the van and tell people we were going to the World Vision headquarters on Mamba Point. The US embassy staff had told us not to tell any Liberians the United States was evacuating its people.

On the way to the US embassy, we had to pass through many

checkpoints. The first one went fine. The World Vision emblem on the van was very similar to the UN emblem, and I think this helped us through the checkpoint. Doug sat in the front passenger seat, looking official with an African driver, and the rest of us sat in the back.

The second checkpoint was just several rocks and sticks in the road. A soldier approached the van, and he was obviously under the influence of drugs. He ordered us out of the van and accused us of transporting weapons for the rebels. I was positive we were about to be killed when Doug bluffed him into believing he was a friend of Daniel Chea, one of Charles Taylor's top advisors and a notorious killer. Doug showed the soldier a business card Chea had given him during a meeting Doug had with Chea two years before. Chea had told Doug to contact him if he ever needed his help. And the soldier let us go. It is unbelievable how God protected us in this situation. We should all be dead. But we made it to the embassy.

Doug and other Americans and Europeans were evacuated from Monrovia that June by the French military, who had a ship just off the Ivory Coast. For Liberians, the fighting was horrible. We Liberians called the fighting in 2000 World War I and the fighting in 2003 World War II. The final fighting in July of 2003 was so terrible we called it World War III—if you added the horrors of WWI to the horrors of WWII, you would be close to the complete horror of WWIII. Thousands of Monrovians died in the July and August fighting in the capital. Finally, the US ambassador to Liberia was able to broker a peace agreement between Charles Taylor's government forces and the LURD and MODEL rebel groups, and there was a break in the fighting.

Taylor had been under tremendous pressure to leave Liberia from the international community, the Women in White, the African Union Leadership, the rebels, and the president of the United States, George W. Bush, and it was part of the terms of the peace agreement arranged by the US ambassador to Liberia that Taylor step down as president and leave Liberia. Charles Taylor finally stepped down as president on August 11, 2003, and left Liberia for Nigeria, where he had been offered political asylum.

The day Charles Taylor stepped down as president will be remembered in Liberia for a long time. People filled the streets of Monrovia singing songs of emancipation. However, because government soldiers were still in control of much of Monrovia, some people hid their joy. They were afraid if Taylor's former soldiers saw them celebrating his departure, they would kill them.

The United Nations sent fifteen thousand troops to Liberia to prevent more fighting. It was the largest contingent of UN peace keeping forces anywhere in the world at the time. Peace had finally come again to Liberia, and we were thankful. But the cost to all of us could never be measured.

After the war ended in August 2003, the AGC Sinkor District and 15 Gate schools were reopened. The Sinkor school is still operating in the Sinkor District of Monrovia, located on the beach of the Atlantic Ocean. Now it is a three-story building with approximately 1,500 square feet per floor, with one small outbuilding and a couple of lean to additions, a latrine building, a well, and a generator for electricity. Water for the school is drawn from the well by a hand pump. The public water system also occasionally works during the day.

After the war, it became very difficult for the AGC board to bring in enough money to support these two schools. The sad truth was, many people in the US thought the crisis in Liberia was over, so they were not as likely to give. The lack of funding was a difficult challenge for me, because I was the director for the schools in Liberia. The money the board was able to send could not cover the payroll for the entire staff, and we were behind on payroll for more than four months.

We appealed desperately to the staff to stay on the job in spite of this, because we were right in the middle of the school year. AGC had a food grant from the UN World Food Program, so we were able to pay the teachers in food, because food was still often impossible to find. Some staff members still made the decision to leave, but we were able to fill these positions because so many teachers were looking for work.

The teachers' salaries were cut from seventy-five US dollars per month to twenty-five or even fifteen US dollars per month plus the World Food Program food allowance. Things were so bad that most of our staff had to find other work to try to feed their families. Most of the time, I personally provided materials, such as chalk and stationery, for the schools.

My cousin, Kebbah, in Boston, Massachusetts, helped me a lot during these hard times. She would ship containers filled with things I could sell in Liberia, such as cosmetics, clothing, and tools. I would sell these items to local merchants and use my profits to buy school supplies. I also would sometimes purchase Liberian products, such as Liberian clothing and jewelry, and ship them to Kebbah.

The AGC board, with help from other volunteers, started more vigorous fundraising efforts and began to bring in more money. Slowly, our financial situation improved, and we were able to pay our teachers again and hire more staff.

The Civil Compound school had been located in a very rural area of Liberia inside the Firestone Plantation where no school had ever existed. It was completely destroyed in the fighting in 2003. Doug and I visited the site of this school in 2004 with an escort from the United Nations, because the area was not yet considered secure. There was nothing left of the school.

However, so great was the desire for education in the area, five classes were still meeting in a nearby one-room church of about eight hundred square feet. Over one hundred children were crammed into this space, and there were separate blackboards for each class. The students had no supplies, and the teachers had no textbooks. The teachers gathered their classes around a blackboard, and the children memorized each lesson from the board. These teachers were the only hope in the world these children had for an education. It was a very emotional moment for Doug and me, as well as for the UN soldiers who accompanied us.

In 2004, I was blessed with a visa for Caleb and myself to travel to the United States. Caleb and I had not seen Rebecca and Joshua since they had left Liberia in 2002. At first, Caleb did not remember his mother, and he cried so hard every time I left him alone with Rebecca. This made Rebecca understandably sad; her youngest son did not know his mother. Eventually, he did accept her, and they grew close again. Caleb's third birthday was celebrated in the US in the presence of Rebecca, Joshua, and myself. We were able to spend almost five months together as a family.

In early 2005, I had to return to Liberia with Caleb, and it was very emotional for Rebecca, Joshua, and myself. Joshua was still young and very happy to be with his younger brother and both parents. We wanted to be together as a family, but we could not. It was overwhelming.

Caleb and I could not legally stay in the US because we only had visitor visas, and I had also made a promise to the US embassy staff member responsible for issuing our visas that I would return to my country along with my son Caleb. I wanted to live by my words. In addition, I had committed long before to continue to help Liberian children affected by the war and give them an education. I had friends like Doug, Nathan, Doug's sister, Barbara, and many other Americans who were supporting the AGC schools in Liberia. I wanted to live by my words, too, that I would continue to help child soldiers and other children affected by the war in Liberia.

And leaving Caleb in the US with Rebecca would have been too difficult and stressful. Rebecca's US visa was a student visa, which meant she could not work in the US to support both her boys and herself, and we did not want to take unfair advantage of our friends who were supporting Rebecca and Joshua by adding three-year-old Caleb. We did not want to destroy our good reputation with our friends and supporters in the US or with the US embassy in Liberia.

Still, we found ourselves in a valley of conflict. Liberia was still a war-torn place: there was still fighting going on in some parts of the country, the poverty rate was debilitating, there were not many doctors, there was little medicine, safe drinking water was scarce, and food was still hard to find. There was no real security. Many people wanted to leave the country or just die. Now that God had helped us to come to the United States, how could I take my small son back to Liberia? This and many other thoughts were running through my mind.

Some of our family back home heard I was planning to bring Caleb back with me, so they called Rebecca and told her not to allow me to bring her son back to Liberia. But Rebecca agreed with me that I had to take Caleb back. She said, "The same God who has been taking care of you in Liberia all this time will still take care of you when you go back." So the decision was finally made, in spite of our fears. I am very grateful to God and to my wife.

I cannot explain how our family looked the day of my and Caleb's departure. It was stress, stress, and more stress. But Caleb and I did get on our flight back to Liberia.

We made a stop in Ghana, where many Liberians had fled during the war and would come to the airport to pass letters to people traveling to Liberia to give to their friends and family there. I knew many of the Liberians standing in the crowd. Some of them asked me, "Why are you taking this child back to hell?" They said I was a fool and one of the stupidest men ever. When we arrived at Roberts International Airport in Liberia, I was told the same thing by friends.

They said, in the Liberian way, "My man, you stupid, oh. You bring this baby from Little Heaven (America) to hell? You crazy, man."

People were staring at me, and some were laughing, while some were mad at me for bringing my own son back to Liberia.

I did not get mad at them; I knew where they were coming from. They did not care to know the reasons why I had to bring Caleb back, and even if I had told them my reasons, they would not have agreed with me, so I decided to just keep quiet, collect our luggage, and head back to Monrovia.

My family members back in Monrovia were also all very upset with me. My older daughter, Martha (my niece who I adopted after my brother died), my sister, Marion, her husband, her four children, and my nephew, James (Martha's brother), who all lived at our home in Matadi were so angry with me for bringing Caleb back. I remember one of my sisters told me that if Caleb died in Liberia, I was going to be blamed for that. I wish they had known what I was going through, but like others, they did not care what my reasons were. Many people could not make the choice Rebecca and I did, but we had good reasons for making it.

It was heartbreaking to take Caleb away from his mother and away from the United States back to Liberia. It would be four more years before we would be reunited as a family in the US and be able to all live there together.

This is my advice to those of you who are reading this story: be honest with yourself and with God and with your fellow human beings. Always seek the Lord in all that you do and want to do: "But seek first his kingdom and his righteousness, and all these things will be given to you as well" (Matthew 6:33). God will give us everything we need for this life if we look to Him first. Romans 8:28 says, "And we know that in all things God works for the good of those who love him, who have been called according to his purpose." God is good to His people. We need to learn to trust God in all matters, even in the very difficult times.

In 2006, three years after the war ended, All God's Children purchased two acres of land for a new 15 Gate school. In 2012, we raised funds in the United States to build a six-room building on this site, which doubled our student capacity at 15 Gate. Now over 350 children are served at the 15 Gate school. 15 Gate is the only school in the area, and some of the students walk three hours one way to get there. The school's staff estimates that there are 250 more school age children living in the surrounding community who have no other access to education. There is a long waiting list.

And although Liberia was still devastated from the war, AGC was able to reopen the Civil Compound school in 2009. AGC obtained a $30,000 grant from ZOE, a Belgian organization, and built six classrooms, offices for the teachers and principal, and a well and a latrine. The school now serves over two hundred children. The local people wanted to be involved in their children's education so much, they donated the land and helped with the construction. In 2014, we started partnering with a Canadian organization called Provision of Hope to teach more effective agriculture methods to the students at Civil Compound.

Because the Liberian Civil War lasted fourteen years, most of the children enrolled during the first years of operation of AGC's schools had never experienced anything but war. Their bright eyes and smiles hid a lot of fear. They liked to have visitors hold their hands and hug them. I still enjoy making children laugh and just sitting with them. The older children love to ask mission team members from the US questions about life in the States. Many of the students like go to a Liberian version of a movie theater, which is simply a darkened room with a television and a DVD player, and for a small price, they can watch American movies.

It is sad that these children learn about America from Hollywood's point of view. Their ideas of America are far from reality. They call Liberia Little Hell, and America is Little Heaven. The children see America as their only hope for a better life, and many of them base this view on the Hollywood image they have of the United States. It is AGC's goal to give these children real hope and a solid future for their lives in Liberia. They are the hope for Liberia's recovery. We are educating the future leaders of Liberia.

AGC is a tuition-free school system. However, the public education system is still not free in Liberia. The children are required by law to wear school uniforms, and the costs might be more than a family's total monthly earnings. Add to these costs the costs of testing fees, school supplies, and books, and a family earning from eighty cents to one dollar a day cannot afford to send their child or children to school. Also, because of subsistence living, many families cannot afford to be without a child that could earn a living, even for the sake of an education.

Almost all of our students have only two changes of clothes: their school uniform and one other outfit. They may have one pair of shoes, and they use these for school, or they share shoes with other children for classes. A few of them have one or two toys at home. They sleep on a mat on a mud or cement floor in one room of a building with the rest of their family.

God has shown his goodness by providing the funds necessary for AGC to give these children hope and a future. The Liberian Ministry of Education has rated our teachers as some of the best trained instructors in the country. In addition to meeting their physical and educational needs, AGC's goal is to see students come to Christ and to experience His love and peace. AGC desires to help children grow into confident and productive adults who make valuable contributions to their families and communities.

Remember, my friend, Nathan, once asked me a question. He asked me what I would recommend to somebody who wanted to help the children of Liberia who, at the time, were suffering through the trauma of devastating civil war. My answer was education. Why? Because much of the other help given to a person will not last; but an education will stay with them for life. Food may run out, clothes may turn to rags or be looted by rebels, but no rebel soldier can ever take education from anyone.

Though my family and I presently live in the United States, we have not forgotten or ever will forget where we have come from and what God has done for us. We are still very involved in the All God's Children schools in Liberia, and as the director for schools in Liberia for AGC, I continue to travel to Liberia for several months at a time every year. I am blessed to help Liberian children become educated and trained up for their own futures and the future of Liberia.

I thank God for His care and His many blessings.

12 ~ RECONCILIATION

In the same way education is so important for future generations of Liberians, reconciliation is vital for the future of the entire country. But even though the Liberian Civil War ended in 2003, reconciliation between former combatants and civilians continues to be a challenge for Liberians because of the trauma and devastation we endured. We still have not recovered.

- An estimated 10 percent of the population (250,000 people) died during the fourteen-year civil war. Many of these were non-combatants.
- According to the CIA World Fact Book (July 2016), over 63 percent of Liberia's 4.1 million people live in poverty. The literacy rate is 47.6 percent, life expectancy is 58.6 years, and there is 1 doctor for every 100,000 people. The unemployment rate is about 85 percent.
- Most of Liberia still does not have basic utility services, such as running water or electricity. The land based telephone system was destroyed, there is no more postal system, and buses and trains no longer operate. There is little safe drinking water or sanitation.

How can Liberia work toward reconciliation and a future in these post-war conditions?

The new Liberian government's first step toward moving forward after the war was to set up the Truth and Reconciliation Commission of Liberia (TRC). The TRC's mandate was to promote peace, security, and reconciliation. The TRC set out to find the root causes of the civil war and determine responsibility for the abuses committed over those fourteen years.[11] As part of

11. "Truth Commission: Liberia," United States Institute of Peace, accessed May 18, 2017, https://www.usip.org/publications/2006/02/truth-commission.

their investigation, the commissioners of the TRC sought to create a record of the mayhem Liberia experienced from 1989 to 2003. They conducted interviews with both victims and perpetrators.

In 2008, Karin Brulliard wrote an article for the January 5 edition of the Washington Post entitled "Area Liberians Recount Horrors for the Commission." In the article, Robin Phillips, executive director of Minnesota Advocates for Human Rights, states that the TRC commissioners decided the project could only be accurate if it also included testimonies from the thousands of Liberians who fled the country to escape the fighting. However, many Liberians at home and abroad continue to remain silent about what they saw and experienced during the war.

Many people want to forget the war and get on with their lives. Some are afraid others will find out they were combatants who took part in terrorizing communities across Liberia and seek revenge. There are those who regret not speaking out against what was happening when they had a chance in the early days of the conflict and struggle with the knowledge their silence might have cost the lives of innocent people. Many simply do not want to trigger flashbacks and nightmares.

In her article, Brulliard interviewed Edwin Lloyd, a Liberian now living in Minnesota. This is what Lloyd said about the war:

Near the bar, Edwin Lloyd, a pastor, sipped juice from a plastic cup and said he was unsurprised by the silence. He has seen it at his Beltsville parish, Whosoever Will Christian Church, where his Liberian congregants sometimes publicly thank God for getting them out alive but mostly don't describe their experiences.

"A lot of them have vivid memories of what transpired," Lloyd, forty-two, said. "I have the mental strength to endure what I saw. A lot of people don't have that."

This is what Lloyd saw, as he walked in a long line of migrants fleeing Monrovia, the capital: Bodies "every ten steps." Fathers killed in front of their children. Starving babies abandoned by mothers who had no food to give them. Rebels who had just beheaded a victim holding up bloody knives like trophies. This is what he heard: the rustling of people being dragged into bushes then the blast of gunfire.

Families were torn apart, and homes and buildings were looted of everything or completely destroyed. Liberia's children were orphaned, tortured, used as child soldiers, and killed. Now these children are young adults, and it is not uncommon to have extended families living under the same roof with a young woman who was raped by fighters and a young man who was a child soldier and committed atrocities himself.

How is reconciliation possible with someone who committed atrocities against friends and family? There are still thirty to forty thousand ex-combatants in Liberia. How do I, as a Christian for example, respond to the ex-combatants I see today in my community? Can I forgive them for what they did?

God has forgiven me, and God Himself has helped me to forgive. Now, I must believe I can help to bring about reconciliation and healing in my country.

Ken Sande of Peacemaker Ministries has written several books about reconciliation. Sande and his associates have used Peacemaker Ministries' four-step process to help families, business associates, and other groups achieve reconciliation. The principles can be modified and applied with success whether or not conflicted parties have Christian backgrounds.

Liberians need true reconciliation with each other, and this four-step process is an excellent model to follow. Liberians can work better together if we have reconciled our differences and we have one common goal to rebuild Liberia. And particularly as Christians, reconciliation is a powerful testimony to the world about the restorative nature of God's love.

Step one: Glorify God. First Corinthians 10:31 says Christians are to glorify God in everything that they do: "So whether you eat or drink or whatever you do, do it all for the glory of God." God is a loving God, and shows us mercy and grace. Jesus tells us to love one another. We bring God glory when we act like He does and love each other. When we shun a former combatant, how does this behavior glorify God? This is a question we Liberians need to ask ourselves.

Step two: Get the plank out of your eye. Matthew 7:3–5 states:

Why do you look at the speck of sawdust in your brother's eye and pay no attention to the plank in your own eye? How can you say to your brother, "Let me take the speck out of your eye," when all the time there is a plank in your own eye? You hypocrite, first take the plank out of your own eye, and then you will see clearly to remove the speck from your brother's eye.

The things many child soldiers were forced to do were horrific, and we do not want to minimize these acts, but all have sinned against God and others (Romans 3:23). Believers in Christ are not perfect, and we need to be honestly dealing with the sin in our own lives as God reveals it so we can see clearly to help others, including former combatants, deal with what they have done.

Step three: Gently restore. Galatians 6:1 states, "Brothers and sisters, if someone is caught in a sin, you who live by the Spirit should restore that person gently. But watch yourselves, or you also may be tempted." Christians need to humbly approach fellow believers who have sin in their lives and attempt to help restore them to a right relationship with God and others. This same principle can be applied directly to how we respond to a child soldier—gently help him take responsibility for his actions and encourage him to come to the Lord for forgiveness and restoration.

Children who were soldiers or who were otherwise traumatized in the Liberian Civil War, and who are now young adults, might have difficulty developing long-term relationships. They might not know what a loving relationship is or how to receive love. At AGC, we believe we must be willing to give of ourselves to these young adults and love them as God loves everyone.

In the case of former child soldiers, this will sometimes involve tough love. As children, they came to see violence as an acceptable way to deal with life. As young adults trying to get along in their communities, they need to know that boundaries for acceptable behavior do exist. A loving environment that includes reasonable boundaries and is based on Christ's love will create a good foundation for healing and restoration.

Step 4: Reconciliation. "Love . . . keeps no record of wrongs" is from 1 Corinthians 13:4–5. It is impossible to continue to judge former child soldiers for their actions during the Liberian Civil War and love them unconditionally at the same time. Christians who work with former child soldiers must take the list of all of their crimes and wipe it from our minds. This is hard to do. However, the way Christians forgive others is like a mirror that reflects what we believe about God's forgiveness in our own lives. If we value God's forgiveness of ourselves, we will more easily forgive others.

Forgiveness is so important in order to move forward. The news agency IRIN reported on the progress of the Liberian Truth and Reconciliation Committee in 2008:

Unusually for a truth commission, Liberia's TRC is permitted to recommend for prosecution individuals deemed responsible for the most serious rights violations. But officials say the most important part is the process itself.

"The public hearings are meant for victims to recount their stories and identify those who committed atrocities against them," said TRC spokesperson Richmond Anderson.

"Subsequently those perpetrators will be called in by the TRC to face their accusers in a forum where, if necessary, *the perpetrators could seek forgiveness*" (Author's emphasis).

One surprising story of forgiveness and reconciliation to follow the Liberian Civil War is that of Joshua Blahyi, General Butt Naked, mentioned earlier for his part in the fighting in Monrovia in April 1996. As General Butt Naked, Blahyi was one of the most notorious killers in the war, and everyone in Liberia still remembers him and his soldiers. Blahyi and many of his troops wore only lace-up boots or tennis shoes and carried machetes into battle—they believed their nudity made them invincible—and this terrified their enemies. Blahyi has said he and his troops are responsible for killing twenty thousand people during the war.

Blahyi earned a reputation for being even more brutal than many other Liberian warlords. He practiced human sacrifice to the Devil before every battle, and he preferred to sacrifice babies, because he believed their deaths promised the greatest amount of protection. After sacrificing a baby or young child, Blahyi would remove the heart so he and his soldiers could eat it.

On January 21, 2008, NBC News carried an Associated Press article about Blahyi. In it, Blahyi states that in 1996, while charging naked into battle, Jesus Christ appeared to him as a blinding light, spoke to him as a son, and told him he would die unless he repented his sins. After this, Blahyi said he confessed his sins and accepted Christ as his Savior. He has spent years visiting the victims of his former life begging for "complete forgiveness" from the families of those he killed. Many people have granted his request, but many others have refused to forgive him.

Blahyi's transition from vicious mass murderer to Christian pastor appears to be completely genuine. When he was called before Liberia's Truth and Reconciliation Commission in 2008 to answer for his crimes, Blahyi made no attempt to dodge blame, like so many other war criminals. Many of the soldiers appearing before the commission stated that they were innocent of any crimes or that they were just following orders. Blahyi's response was different.

Blahyi told the commission his faith instructed him to tell the truth and "the truth will set me free." He has carried that attitude through to the present day. "I believe that God wishes to use me as a sign. No matter how far a person goes, he has the potential to change," Blahyi has said. He sees himself as a symbol of both incomprehensible evil and seemingly impossible redemption, and he seeks to help bring about Liberia's reconciliation.

In the AP article, Blahyi says, "Forgiveness and reconciliation is the way to go." His changed life is a witness to that truth. When he experienced his new birth in Christ, he proved to every former combatant that a new beginning is possible with the power of God and His forgiveness in their hearts. Blahyi has built a mission in Monrovia for former child soldiers who find it overwhelming to reintegrate into their communities. Many ex-combatants are shunned throughout the country, and Blahyi has offered many of them a refuge. His mother cooks meals for them and helps with some of their other needs.

So you can see we have a huge challenge in Liberia when it comes to reconciliation. Even though Blahyi is repentant, many will not forgive him and reconcile with him. And what about ex-combatants who will not take responsibility for what they have done? How do we deal with them? Ken Sande's Peacemaker principles speak to this situation also.

Sande says the repentance of the offending party is key to full reconciliation, but we cannot depend on it for our own closure of the situation. If we look to the offender to make things right, we may be very disappointed and discouraged. Sande says the most important move in reconciliation happens when the offended party moves more deeply toward God and considers what Christ did on the cross.

When we think about what Christ did on the cross and how He gave His life for our sins so we could have eternal life, our view of ourselves changes. Remember, Romans 3:23 says we have all sinned—even the best of us. But Romans 6:23 says, "The gift of God is eternal life in Christ Jesus our Lord." God has shown us His mercy, so as Christians, instead of seeing ourselves as offended parties, we come to see ourselves as the ones who have offended deeply but have also been forgiven deeply. Out of this view of ourselves, and with God's help, we can forgive even those whose repentance is weak.

For my part, God is helping me forgive and reconcile as much as possible with those who have caused me so much pain. Jesus says, "Blessed are the peacemakers" (Matthew 5:9), and God tells us in Romans 12:18, "If it is possible, as far as it depends on you, live at peace with everyone."

13 ~ THE FUTURE OF LIBERIA

The future for Liberia depends on the politicians of Liberia, as well as each individual Liberian citizen. The country is very small and can easily be developed if the natural resources she has are used in a proper manner. Liberia has gold, diamonds, rubber, and other natural resources. Liberia has the largest rubber plantation in the world, operated by the Firestone Natural Rubber Company. I hope and pray our politicians will develop these resources for the people and put Liberia ahead of themselves.

Individual Liberians also need to take the initiative and look to themselves to solve the country's problems and not rely on the United States or the United Nations to solve everything for us. Yes, we still need much help, but we can rebuild our country, and we need to learn to depend on our own abilities to accomplish this. No matter how much money the outside world gives us, if we are not willing to work to rebuild Mama Liberia, she will not prosper.

Also, the sixteen tribes of Liberia need to understand we are all part of one nation. This nation is not for one tribe; every tribe is important and forms a part of the country. An old Liberian proverb says we all come from one banana tree, so let's all get involved in the rebuilding of Liberia.

For now, the first thing we need to start doing is to forgive one another in an honest manner. I hope every Liberian will learn this lesson well: war is not the solution. Hatred and unforgiveness will not help us in any way. These things will only destroy us and our future. Let bygones be bygones. In our own Liberian way, let's stop the cycle of "I will pay my debt," which means "I will get revenge on all those who hurt me, my family, and my loved ones." Forget the past; let it be done with, and forgive those you have considered enemies.

Corruption is another factor in why Liberia has not been able to redevelop and move forward. We must fight corruption with every power. Bribing was rampant during the war, and I believe it is even worse now than at any point during the fighting. During a trip to Liberia in June 2016, Doug and I were driving in downtown Monrovia, and while at a traffic stop, two men attempted to rob us. Doug's quick response prevented them from taking anything, but the truly disturbing part was a Liberian policeman observed the entire attempted robbery and did nothing to stop it and did not attempt to catch the criminals. I believe the robbers bribed him to not get involved.

This has to stop. Our officials and public servants need to be people of integrity.

And my appeal to those reading this story who are not Liberians but want to help is do not just send funds to the government of Liberia but come and make sure the money is used for the right purposes. If any government or organization says they want to build schools, roads, or other developments in Africa, please follow up and make sure the money is spent on what you give it for, because there is too much corruption in Africa, and in Liberia too often, I see aid meant for the common person spent on fancy cars and houses for politicians and people in powerful government positions.

Liberians need to start thinking about and doing what US president John F. Kennedy said long ago: "And so, my fellow Americans: ask not what your country can do for you, ask what you can do for your country." It is not about how much I can take; it is about how much I can give that will make a difference in Liberia. If every Liberian can develop this mind-set, our future will be brighter and greater.

Liberians need to get back to the soil. We need to redevelop our agricultural system and stop relying on imported food supplies to meet our needs. We grew our own rice before the war, and we can do it now.

We also need a better health care system. So many of our clinics and hospitals were destroyed during the war and are still not functioning. We lost so many skilled medical professionals who were killed or fled to other countries. We must rebuild our clinics and hospitals and staff them with trained Liberians.

To reach these goals, Liberia needs a good education system. My desire for our All God's Children schools is to produce faithful, hard-working, future leaders for Liberia. We in Liberia need to train our youth for tomorrow. We need to teach the youth to fish rather than always simply giving them fish to eat. Then they will be able to fish for themselves.

Now that the civil war has been over in Liberia for more than a decade, our AGC student body has greatly changed. In the beginning, we served former combatants and children who lived through the Liberian Civil War. Now we are educating the children born during the war. We need to continue to focus on our students, because they have no other access to quality education, but we also need to consider ways to help their parents by offering vocational training, adult education, and counseling. Liberia needs electricians, carpenters, medical personnel, computer technicians and operators, teachers, tailors, and many other professionals to help rebuild our country. Giving young Liberians these skills will make them more productive, but we will need vocational schools in our communities to help them learn. My prayer and desire for AGC is to also develop such vocational schools to help the development of Liberia's future professionals and tradespeople.

To the United States and the international community, please come and help us rebuild. We want to move forward on our own, but we still need assistance. We are the stepchild of the United States. You helped bring us into being. Do not turn your back on us. Liberians were very disappointed when the US did not come to our aid early on in the war. But we still love and respect the US. Liberia depends on God first and the United States second. Even now, I still often seek funds in the US to help AGC and Liberia and to support the building of vocational schools for our young people.

To all Liberians, the war is over. Let us work together for the common good of Mama Liberia. While the United States and other countries are trying their best to help us, let us learn to work hard alongside these countries and to help Liberia rebuild and move forward. Let us lay aside tribal and political differences and live and work together as one people. Remember, Liberia was once a peaceful country. We were even able to support other African nations in their freedom and independence. We can support ourselves now in the same way. Liberia is down, but with the help of the US and other countries and by the special grace of God, we can learn to stand on our own feet again, together.

14 ~ THE ETHICS OF WAR

The Liberian Civil War was a war visited upon the people of Liberia by warlords. The warlords were greedy for power, and their war was a selfish one. It was not a just war.

Many of my friends joined one or more of the several military factions that fought in Liberia between 1989 and 2003, but I could not take up arms against fellow Liberians, no matter how others justified their actions.

As a believer in Christ, I am instructed to submit to the governing authorities, but what about a Liberian government that was murdering its own people? What about leaders like Samuel Doe and Charles Taylor who killed innocent Liberians and fought their fellow countrymen?

If another country had attacked Liberia, then I would have had a good reason to take up arms—I would have been justified in defending my country. But Liberians were fighting other Liberians, so I refused to fight. Though, it was sometimes hard.

God has instituted government. But Christianity must never become confused with a political movement or with a national government. Christians are not to be identified with murder and assassination or be known as terrorists. They are not to cause havoc upon others or destroy communities. Christians are to be a source of the peace of God.

The believer may resist government if the government is doing things against God's will. We are told by God in the Bible not to shed innocent blood (Jeremiah 22.3), so if I am asked by any government or authority to murder someone, I will not follow that instruction. God does not want me, as a believer, to partake in evil against others.

Liberians like myself, who refused to join the government forces or any of the other factions, can rest assured we were not acting in direct conflict with scripture, because all of the factions were unjust in their actions.

There are several criteria, first developed by Augustine and refined by Aquinas, we can use to discover whether or not a war is just:

1. War in defense of the innocent is just: In the Liberian Civil War, most of the estimated 250,000 deaths were innocent civilians. It was the leaders of the warring factions who committed these crimes against the populace. Even the ECOMOG peacekeepers killed civilians and looted.

2. Wars fought to execute justice are just: I do not believe any of the faction leaders were concerned about justice during the war in Liberia. They were concerned about themselves and what status and wealth they might claim from winning the war, such as the presidency or control of the country's resources.

3. A just war must be fought by a government: Individuals cannot take up arms without the government's consent, but this was the inception and furtherance of the Liberian Civil War. Doe's first violent act of rebellion against the elected government of Tolbert was followed by Taylor's acts of aggression against Doe and so on.

4. A just war must be fought justly: Doe's government was not just, and the factions that fought Doe were not just. It was tribe against tribe, and killings were often based on what tribe a person was from and nothing else. Civilians bore the brunt of all the fighting.

So the Liberian civil war was not a just war.

It has been said war is hell. I have seen war, and I can attest to this as fact. The Bible does not condemn war or condemn a Christian for being involved in the military and in war. However, are we as citizens of our country required to join the military and fight in a war simply because our nation's leaders have claimed the war is just? I cannot agree with this train of thought.

Nowadays, I read about terrorists killing innocent people across the globe and about the impacted nations responding by bombing known terrorist hiding places and accepting the collateral damage that always occurs. But collateral damage is civilians. Somewhere, a terrorist leader was killed, but outside his hiding place was a small shop operated by an innocent civilian, and he was also killed. His wife is now a widow and his children are fatherless. Is this just?

The children of the father who was killed then ask, "Why was my father killed? Who did this to our family?" These children become easy recruits for a terrorist organization. Many lack education and are easily subverted to the causes of terrorists. This is exactly how Charles Taylor recruited children into his army in Liberia. The Small Boy Units that comprised a large part of his forces were children who were mostly uneducated and who were orphaned by the war.

The vicious cycle of killing terrorist leaders and creating more terrorists is not the answer. Only dealing with the root cause of war will stop this cycle. And the root cause of war is sin, sin in the form of selfishness, greed, and rebellion against God and His admonition to love one another.

As a Christian, my life must be a witness to God's love and forgiveness. I need to live the way Christ lived on earth. Living the way Christ lived means loving God and serving and forgiving others. No matter what happens in our lives, we all can choose how to respond, whether it is to a minor problem or a life-threatening event.

When war does invade my life, what do I think and how do I act?

First, I know God loves me and I can trust Him. He gave His own Son so I can have eternal life, and He cares for me every day. As I spend time with Him in prayer and read His Word, I get to know Him better. When trouble of any kind comes, and it will, I can show I love Him by continuing to trust Him and praise Him. Jesus says, "I have told you these things, so that in me you may have peace. In this world, you will have trouble. But take heart! I have overcome the world" (John 16:33).

Second, I can serve others by helping them in their time of trouble and hardship. And you do not need a war or calamity to be available to help those in need. Galatians 6:2 says, "Carry each other's burdens, and in this way, you will fulfill the law of Christ." The law of Christ is love.

We all have burdens. Some have physical handicaps, chronic illnesses, or other abnormalities they cannot change. Some have spiritual burdens. Some have emotional burdens, such as depression or anxiety, heartache over loss, or financial setback. All of us should consider this question: "Who have I comforted recently, and who has comforted me?"

I draw strength from 2 Corinthians 1:3–4, which says, "Praise be to the God and Father of our Lord Jesus Christ, the Father of compassion and the God of all comfort, who comforts us in all our troubles, so that we can comfort those in any trouble with the comfort we ourselves receive from God."

The point of this verse is God is always there to comfort me, and this gives me the desire to comfort others in need. I had many opportunities to do this during the war by praying for people, showing compassion, giving people food or money for food, giving people a place to stay, or leading them to a safe place away from the fighting, even at the risk of my own life. All of these experiences developed in me the ability and desire I have now to help people in their marriages, with their children, and in their times of depression or physical sickness.

God allows sorrows to come to us so we can be comforted and in turn comfort others in need.

The Liberian Civil War, from 1989 to 2003, was not just, but it provided me my own battleground for peace, where I was challenged to practice the love I have learned and a doctrine of mercy and selflessness. And God brought me through.

EPILOGUE: WHERE IS GOD IN WAR?

We have asked the question, where is God in war? As you have read my story, you have seen He has always been right there with me, no matter what I was going through. You have seen that He was working through the lives of people who helped me throughout my life. You have also seen how He blessed me with good things, even in the midst of trouble.

Sometimes I could see God working through other people in my life, and other times I did not understand what He was doing. My first aunty I lived with as a young boy was very hard on me. But God used these experiences to prepare me for the hardship and trauma of war. On the other hand, God brought Pastor Dennis Gaye into my life when I was going down the destructive path of gambling, drugs, and sex. This man loved me so much and helped me see how God loves me. He was patient and persistent, because he wanted me to have a better life here on earth and eternal life after. He wanted what God wanted for me. He lived out Jesus's love for me and my family.

Then there was General Satan. I knew this man before the war, and he lived with me at our church in the clinic before he was a soldier. When my family and I were at Greystone during the terrible April 1996 fighting, I became very depressed because of what my family was going through. I felt there was nothing I could do to help them, and I went so low I just wanted to die. I went outside the compound so the rebel soldiers could kill me. But General Satan appeared and spared me. I wanted to die, but God used a man called Satan to save my life.

God had other plans for me. He wanted to use my life to help others.

God continued to bless me, even while I was going through all kinds of trouble during the war. The war had been going on for about three years when I met Rebecca, my wife. This woman loves God and her family. She is always giving of herself to serve other people. We have been through war, loss of loved ones, and separation from each other and our children, along with all the normal ups and downs that come with being married and raising a family. In all these things, Rebecca and my children have been a great blessing from God.

God also blessed me with the desire to help Liberia's children and the opportunity to act on this desire. When we started our first All God's Children school, it was an answer to my prayers. All through the war years and beyond, I have been able to give former child soldiers and other traumatized children education, guidance, and encouragement. With God's help, I have been able to show them that someone still cares about them, and I have provided them an example to follow in their lives.

I have seen God working in me to help me forgive people who have mistreated me. Instead of holding on to my anger and being bitter, with God's help, I have been able to forgive my aunty for the years of abuse. I have been able to forgive the soldiers who made life so hard for my family and caused me so much pain. God is helping me become more like my example, Jesus, who is forgiving. As He was hanging on the cross, He said, "Father, forgive them, for they do not know what they are doing" (Luke 23:34).

God was always there with me, giving me strength to go on. God was there, working through people who helped me. He was there, blessing me in the midst of trouble. He was there, giving me opportunities to care for others and helping me forgive those who wronged me.

Where is God in war? Right beside me, where He always is.

APPENDIX I

Christians should be deeply concerned about war and its devastation. War reeks of death, destruction, personal loss, and nightmares. Consider these facts: Between 1990 and 1995, there were seventy nations at war. More than five million people died in these conflicts. More than three-quarters of those killed were civilians.

The root cause of war can be traced back to the book of Genesis and what the Bible calls sin. Genesis chapters 1 and 2 describe a world at peace. Human beings did not shed blood, even the blood of animals. They had no knowledge of evil in the world God first created. God gave Adam and Eve everything to meet their needs and more. They enjoyed wholesome food, clean air and water, no sickness, purpose and fulfillment, and eternal life in relationship with God. Adam and Eve's fall changed this. They made the decision to disobey God by eating the fruit from the tree of the knowledge of good and evil, and this was the birth of sin.

God told them if they ate from this tree, they would certainly die, and He wanted them to experience life, not death. They decided to follow God's enemy, Satan, and their own way instead of trusting what God had told them was good and true. They learned about sin through experience and learned sin brings death and destruction to life and relationships. Adam and Eve's perfect relationship with God was broken, and the consequences would affect every generation thereafter. Sin is not simply a single bad action. It is like poison.

In Genesis chapter 3, the Bible shows, because of sin, violence and death entered human experience. God's enemy, Satan, was against humankind from the beginning, and worked to bring death and destruction into our lives. However, God Himself has provided the remedy. In response to Satan's actions against Adam and Eve, God said to Satan, "And I will put enmity between you and the woman, and between your offspring and hers; he will crush your head, and you will strike his heel" (Genesis 3:15). Satan would be permitted to afflict Christ in His humanness and bring suffering on God's people (strike his heel). But the serpent's poison is in its head, and to crush a serpent's head is to kill it. Satan received that fatal blow from Christ on the cross. Christ atoned for our sin, died, and was resurrected, and the poisonous power of sin and death over human beings has been crushed. We can now live in relationship with God without fear of death, knowing we have been gifted eternal life.

With Christ as our Savior, we do not need to let sin master us, and we look forward to a time when sin will again be gone completely from the world.

We see how the consequences of sin progressed even further in the lives of Cain and Abel, Adam and Eve's sons. Genesis chapter 4 tells how they brought their offerings to the Lord. God accepted Abel's offering but did not accept Cain's. Cain was very angry about this, but God told him he would be accepted if he did what was right. God, in His love for Cain, also warned him if he did not do what was right, "Sin is crouching at your door; it desires to have you, but you must rule over it" (Genesis 4:7).

God gave Cain a chance to turn away from his anger and self-centeredness, but Cain rejected God's warning and held onto his anger toward God and his jealousy toward his brother, Abel. Cain invited Abel out into a field and murdered him. God wanted Cain to have good relationships with Him and with his family and be happy, fulfilled, and at peace within himself. Instead, Cain's sinful anger and jealousy festered and brought about death and broken relationships.

Conflict, and ultimately war, are the results of sin entering the world and sin in human hearts. Greed, jealousy, anger, revenge, hunger for power and status in an individual or a group: all these can lead to war. And there are times when a nation must defend itself against those who attack out of these sinful motivations. However, our God is one of peace. Just as He can bring peace to the human heart and peace between individuals in this world, one day He will bring peace again to the whole earth.

We see this clearly in Isaiah 2:1–4. Isaiah tells us about life in the new heaven and new earth after Jesus returns:

In the last days, the mountain of the Lord's temple will be established as the highest of the mountains; it will be exalted above the hills, and all nations will stream to it. Many peoples will come and say, "Come, let us go up to the mountain of the Lord, to the temple of the God of Jacob. He will teach us his ways so that we may walk in his paths." The law will go out from Zion, the word of the Lord from Jerusalem. He will judge between the nations and will settle disputes for many peoples. They will beat their swords into plowshares and their spears into pruning hooks. Nation will not take up sword against nation, nor will they train for war anymore.

We have seen sin creates lack of peace on three levels: Sin keeps us from having a relationship with God, what the Bible calls peace with God, "Therefore, since we have been justified through faith, we have peace with God through our Lord Jesus Christ" (Romans 5:1). Sin robs us of inner peace through jealousy, dissatisfaction, and bitterness in our hearts. And finally, sin leads to conflict between individuals and groups.

When it comes to war, war is of humanity's making, not God's. Our wars should not be fought in the name of God. Wars are started because people are sinful and selfish. Because of this, we can't *all just get along*. There is always someone who wants more at the expense of others, who hates, or who attacks out of fear or revenge, whether on a tribal or global scale.

Wars may be fought on the battlefields of the world, but they are first waged in our hearts. I believe most of us clearly recognize the tragedy of war, and no one can argue that any war is good. But we can say that war in most cases could be avoided if sin in some form was not the overpowering factor. In the Liberian Civil War, greed over the natural resources of diamonds, gold, and timber and the thirst for power were contributing sinful factors.

God does wage one war, but it is not a physical one; it is the war for people's hearts.

God cares for every person. The key to real personal peace is not found in who has the biggest gun, but in relationship with Jesus Christ. Remember, Jesus tells His followers in John 14:27, "Peace I leave with you; my peace I give you. I do not give to you as the world gives. Do not let your hearts be troubled, and do not be afraid." We can only find true peace by trusting in Jesus Christ. Christians need to share this Source of true peace with the world.

Christians cannot control the world around us, but we serve an all-powerful God who is in control and who will bring peace in His own time. However, we can positively impact the people that God brings into our lives. God has purposely placed us where we are. We can evidence His peace in our lives and pursue peace with others. He has given us the passion, power, and talents we need, and He calls us to carry out His purpose, sharing the Good News of eternal life and peace in Christ.

APPENDIX II

What should a Christian's attitude be toward fighting in a war? If the government orders its young men and women to join the military and fight, what options do we, as Christians, have?

In Titus 3:1, Paul tells Titus to "remind the people to be subject to rulers and authorities, to be obedient." Peter also talks about a Christian's responsibility to obey the government: "Be subject for the Lord's sake to every human institution, whether it be to the emperor as supreme or to governors sent by him" (1 Peter 2:13–14).

What is the relationship between believers and the state? Romans 13:1–2 seems to make it clear all believers should be subject to government authority, because all authority comes from God:

Let everyone be subject to the governing authorities, for there is no authority except that which God has established. The authorities that exist have been established by God. Consequently, whoever rebels against the authority is rebelling against what God has instituted, and those who do so will bring judgment on themselves.

It does not matter how civil authorities were appointed or by whom. The authority, whether just or unjust, whether legitimate or illegitimate, is to be obeyed because God has established all government. Keep in mind, the infamous Nero was ruling as the emperor of Rome when God led Paul to give these instructions.

There are three institutions ordained by God: the family, the church, and the government. All three exist because God set them up as the means by which people are to relate to each other and to Him as God. It is God's will that government exist and that persons have the authority to rule within the state.

However, the sphere of authority a government has must be clearly understood. The government has authority only within the *civil realm*; it is not all-encompassing. The authority God grants in any area of society does not extend beyond its position. For example, when Paul commands wives to obey their husbands in Ephesians 5:22, they are required to obey them as *husbands*, not as masters or as kings. Children are to obey their parents as *parents*, not as sovereign rulers (Ephesians 6:1). It is the same in the case of government leaders. Government is ordained by God, but men and women in leadership positions are responsible for how they carry out their functions.

Each of these three institutions, the family, the church, and the government, has those in authority who are faithful and do an excellent job. Each also has those serving at various levels who are totally disobedient to God and do a terrible job. The fact to remember is government is ordained by God, and rulers are answerable to Him; they shall give an account to God.

However, the thrust of Romans 13:1–2 is not about government leaders and their responsibilities; the thrust is believers and their duty to the state. Usually, believers can do little about how government authorities conduct their affairs, but believers can do a great deal about their behavior as citizens within the state. God is very clear about believers' behavior: as followers of Christ, we are to be the salt and light of the world.

In Luke 3, John the Baptist answers questions about living a life following God. Luke 3:14 says, "Then some soldiers asked him, 'And what should we do?'" In other words, how do we as soldiers live the way God wants us to live?

John does not condemn the vocation of the soldiers or tell them to leave the army. Being soldiers does not keep them from having a relationship with God. Instead, John says, "Don't extort money and don't accuse people falsely—be content with your pay." John tells them to live an honest life and to not use their power and position to take advantage of other people. It is how soldiers live their lives that shows they are following God.

Believers who resist the authorities will bring judgment on themselves, as it states in Romans 13:2 above. The idea is disobedient believers will have to face the judgment of God if they disobey the just laws of a government. Some commentators think this also refers to the judgment of the civil authorities. There is no question, if believers are caught breaking the laws of the state, they will be punished. However, the civil authorities may never catch disobedient believers; but God knows every law broken by believers, and by resisting the laws of the state, believers break the law of God.

I will admit a possible exception to not resisting government is allowed believers. When rulers begin to exercise personal and immoral mastery over human life, believers are to obey God and not man. Believers are always to follow after righteousness, that is, morality and justice. However, note a crucial point: the morality and justice pursued by believers must be the morality and justice of God's Word and not of man's making. We must look to God and the Bible for answers, not to our own sense of justice.

In Exodus 1, Hebrew midwives disobey the government of Egypt by not killing male Hebrew babies. This is a clear example of divinely approved disobedience to government authorities (see also Daniel 3 and Daniel 6). Christians need to put God before the government. We must encourage obedience to government, but we have the right to disobey oppressive commands. However, we must also be ready to take the consequences the government may bring against us if we do so.

Acts 5:29 says, "Peter and the other apostles replied: 'We must obey God rather than human beings!'" This suggests to us there are times when the laws of man go against the laws of God. If believers know a war goes against the teachings of God, they have the right to refuse to fight in obedience to a higher power.

We need to be very concerned about our motives when making these decisions, however. They cannot be made lightly. They are not a matter of whether or not we agree with a particular war, for example. Our decisions must go much deeper than that. The war must go against a clear command of God. Only then do we have a right to refuse to go to war.

Early church leaders, from Augustine (AD 354-430) to Thomas Aquinas (AD 1225-1274), taught the Just War Doctrine. This doctrine explains the conditions under which a Christian may participate in a war. The view that all war is wrong does not come from scripture. Exodus 20:13 states, "You shall not murder." This command does not prohibit all forms of killing. Capital punishment, self-defense, and killing enemy soldiers during war are not murder. There is no doubt I would defend my family at all costs if someone attempted to harm them.

For example, millions of children have grown up learning the story of David and how he killed Goliath. David was a man "after God's own heart" (Acts 13:22), but he was also a man of war. Before David killed Goliath, a servant introduced David to Saul in 1 Samuel 16:18: "One of the servants answered, 'I have seen a son of Jesse of Bethlehem who knows how to play the lyre. He is a brave man and a warrior. He speaks well and is a fine-looking man. And the Lord is with him.'"

In Psalm 44:4–7 David writes:

You are my King and my God, who decrees victories for Jacob. Through you we push back our enemies; through your name we trample our foes. I put no trust in my bow, my sword does not bring me victory; but you give us victory over our enemies, you put our adversaries to shame.

David was a trained warrior at a young age, and the Lord was with him. David recognized his military victories over the enemies of God's people were from God.

As Christians, war is not forbidden to us, and we are subject to worldly authority, but we are subject to God first.

BIBLIOGRAPHY

Associated Press, "Liberian General with Racy Moniker Confesses: Rebel Commander Known as Gen. Butt Naked Admits Killing Thousands," *NBC News*, January 21, 2008, http://www.nbcnews.com/id/22765054/ns/world_news-africa/t/liberian-general-racy-moniker-confesses/#.WUrmMGxK3ic.

Brulliard, Karen, "Area Liberians Recount Horrors for Commission," *Washington Post*, January 5, 2008, http://www.washingtonpost.com/wp-dyn/content/article/2008/01/04/AR2008010403687.html.

Davis, John J. *Evangelical Ethics*. Phillipsburg: P&R Publishing, 2004.

Ellis, Stephen. *The Mask of Anarchy*. New York: New York University Press, 2001.

Geisler, Norman L. *Christian Ethics*. Grand Rapids: Baker Books, 2002.

Kulah, Arthur F. *Liberia Will Rise Again*. Nashville: Abingdon Press, 1999.

Pham, John-Peter. *Liberia: Portrait of a Failed State*. New York: Reed Press, 2004.

Sande, Ken. *The Peacemaker*. Grand Rapids: Baker Books, 2004.

"Truth Commission Seeks Answers to 1979–2003 Strife," *IRIN*, January 10, 2008, http://www.irinnews.org/report/76174/liberia-truth-commission-seeks-answers-1979-2003-strife.

Williams, Gabriel. *Liberia: The Heart of Darkness*. Victoria: Trafford Publishing, 2002.

MAPS

MAP OF LIBERIA WITHIN AFRICA

1. Kakata
2. 15 Gate
3. Roberts Field
4. Harbel
5. Paynesville

MAP OF MONROVIA WITHIN LIBERIA

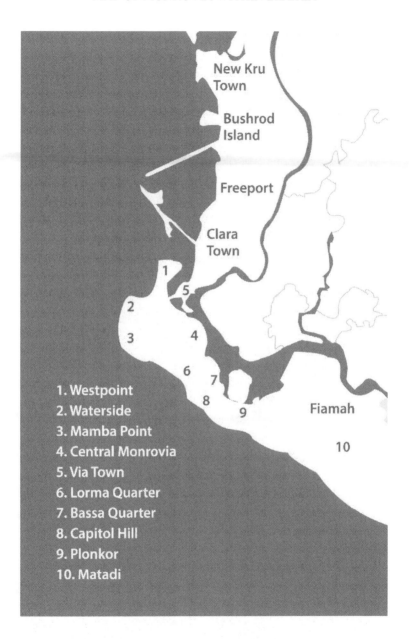

New Kru Town

Bushrod Island

Freeport

Clara Town

1

5

2

3

4

6

7

8

9

Fiamah

10

1. Westpoint
2. Waterside
3. Mamba Point
4. Central Monrovia
5. Via Town
6. Lorma Quarter
7. Bassa Quarter
8. Capitol Hill
9. Plonkor
10. Matadi

ABOUT THE AUTHORS

Sackie Kwalalon has been the Liberia country director of All God's Children Schools since its inception in 1997. He is also the founder and general overseer of the Word of Faith Bible Church in Liberia. A pastor and educator, he has invested in countless lives, bringing hope and wisdom to help people of all ages grow and flourish. Sackie was born and raised in Liberia and endured the horrific fourteen-year Liberian Civil War. He knows that education is crucial for each child's development, and for the future generations of Liberia. He divides his time between his home in the Tacoma area and his home in Liberia, where he oversees the AGC schools and their community involvement. Sackie and his wife have two children.

Doug Collier is a cofounder of All God's Children Schools in Liberia. He is the board president of Serve the Children, the supporting organization of All God's Children Schools. A CPA and financial planner, he also has a doctorate of ministry in strategic leadership from Faith International Seminary in Tacoma. He has traveled to Liberia regularly since his first trip in 1997. Doug's passion is to come alongside educators in Liberia with long-term support as they help children and their families toward a better future. As a part of this support, he leads mission teams to Liberia and can attest to the life-changing effects of these missions in the lives of Liberian children, the in-country AGC staff, and the team members themselves. Doug and his wife live in the Tacoma area and have two married children and five grandchildren.

Serve the Children
4423 Pt Fosdick Drive NW #202
Gig Harbor, WA 98335
www.servethechildren.com

Made in the USA
Lexington, KY
12 December 2019

58492543R00096